How to
Tarot Cards

How to Read Your Tarot Cards

Discover the Tarot and Find Out
What Your Cards Really Mean

LIZ DEAN

CICO BOOKS
London New York

Please note that Tarot cards are intended to be treated responsibly and with respect. Generally, they are not suitable for children. The way one reads Tarot cards may be guided by the information in this kit, but ultimately the interpretation of the cards is up to the individual, for which neither the publisher nor author can be held accountable.

First published as *The Mystery of the Tarot* in Great Britain in 2003 by Cico Books Ltd

This edition published in the United States in 2007 by Cico Books
an imprint of Ryland, Peters & Small Ltd
519 Broadway, 5th Floor, New York, NY 10012

10 9 8 7 6 5 4 3 2 1

Text copyright © Liz Dean 2003, 2007
Design & illustration © Cico Books 2003, 2007

The author's moral rights have been asserted. All rights reserved. No part of this publication may be reproduced, stored in a retrieval system, or transmitted in any form or by any means, electronic, mechanical, photocopying, or otherwise, without the prior permission of the publisher.

A CIP record for this title is available from the Library of Congress

ISBN-10: 1 904991 81 5
ISBN-13: 978 1 904991 81 6

Printed in China

Design: David Fordham
Editor: Mandy Greenfield

Contents

Introduction 6

1 Tarot Traditions 8
Court and Clergy: Europe's First Tarot 8   Tarot as Trade 10
Knights and Gypsies 12   The Origins of the Minor Arcana 14
The Occult Revival: Egyptomania 16

2 Tarot Symbolism 20
Using Astrology with the Tarot 20   The Tarot and Kabbala 24
The Tarot Menagerie 28   The Tarot Rainbow 30

3 How to Lay the Cards 32
Tarot Readings 32   Three-card Readings 36   The Heart and
Head Spread 38   The Star Spread 40   The Past, Present and
Future Spread 42   The Celtic Cross 45   The Tree of Life
Spread 48   The Horseshoe Spread 51   The Year Ahead Spread 53
The Month Ahead Spread 56   The Week Ahead Spread 58
What to Do if You Cannot Make Sense of a Reading 61

4 Interpreting the Cards

The Major Arcana 62
The Minor Arcana 110

Tarot Resources 155
Index 158
Acknowledgements 160

Introduction

The TAROT IS A STORY, as all good mysteries are. Its reputation has the romance of the Romanies, the power of the Italian dukes who commissioned the first cards, and a 600-year-long popularity. One episode saw the cards being carried by persecuted missionaries as a secret code; another twist had the Tarot denounced by the Church as "the devil's picture book." Yet universally the Tarot has been a tool for those seeking enlightenment.

There is no end to the Tarot saga, for whenever the cards are consulted and laid out in a spread, a new story begins. The narrative is never rigid, because the events revealed in a reading reflect the nature of our own thoughts and actions, which constantly change. The cards themselves do not create events; we have the autonomy to emphasize any aspect which they highlight.

Learning Tarot is like learning a language, but it uses symbols as a way to explain itself. The occultist A. E. Waite, in his *Pictorial Key to the Tarot*, says: "Given the inward meaning of its emblems, [the cards] do become a kind of alphabet which is capable of indefinite combinations and makes true sense in all."

It is hoped that this book inspires you to learn how to use the Tarot and benefit from the insight that this ancient mirror of life provides.

ABOVE: *The Sun, from the Classic Tarot, 1835. The engravings are by the Italian artist Carlo Della Rocca, whose work was famous in the nineteenth century.*

INTRODUCTION

How to Use This Book

The first chapter presents a history of Tarot cards. It suggests the threads of their mystery, from what are possibly the oldest surviving cards—the fifteenth-century Visconti-Sforza—to the evolution of the esoteric decks created from the 1700s onward. At this time, connections between the kabbala (an ancient Jewish mystical tradition) and astrology were established, and these are also examined in this section.

The second chapter shows you how to lay out the cards for a reading, ranging from the simplest three-card spread to more detailed layouts, such as the Celtic Cross and the Tree of Life. There are examples of genuine readings to demonstrate how the cards work in action, and how they relate to—and illuminate—each other during interpretation.

Chapter three offers interpretations for all seventy-eight cards: the twenty-two cards of the major arcana and the fifty-six of the minor arcana. For the major arcana there is a passage on the card's symbolism, and another that decodes the astrological symbols that appear on many Tarot decks. The historical deck shown is the Visconti-Sforza Tarot; the modern deck is *The Art of Tarot* deck (see pages 4 and 155 for further details). Each interpretation presents card combinations and some include a historical anecdote, so that you can see how specific cards work in conjunction with one another or delve deeper into the origins of salient cards.

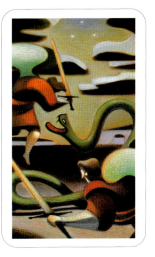

ABOVE: *Some Tarot decks are inspired by the work of well-known artists, such as the Giotti and Salvador Dali Tarots. The card above is from the Dante Tarot, created by Andrea Serio.*

The card interpretations for the minor arcana are grouped by their number, each with an introduction explaining their numerology. Learning the card numerologies can be a valuable shortcut when reading the numbered (or "pip") cards, particularly if your deck has geometric designs rather than illustrated pips. The Court cards (or "Face cards") are also grouped together. Their introductions help explain how these cards act as energies, as well as representing specific people; for the beginner, the Court cards can be notoriously difficult to relate to, if they are considered solely as personalities.

Turn to page 155 for recommended websites and some Tarot "bibles," whose authors I thank here for making the deeper study of this subject, and its practice, so enjoyable.

7

1 TAROT TRADITIONS
COURT AND CLERGY: EUROPE'S FIRST TAROT

PAGAN, EGYPTIAN, KABBALISTIC, early Christian, satanic: these terms have all been used to describe the ancient system of divination that is Tarot. Yet these descriptions really relate to the user more than they do to the cards themselves.

This can be seen in the myriad decks that are available today: there is the Arthurian Tarot and the Tarot of the Witches; the Salvador Dali deck and the Jung-based Mythic Tarot; the Tantra, Ukiyoe, and Osho Zen Tarots; the Tarot of the Sphinx, Tarot of the Cat People, Motherpeace Tarot, and Aleister Crowley's Book of Thoth; along with numerous astrological Tarots, fairy Tarots, love Tarots, and I Ching cards. All seek to explain the mystery of Tarot through a host of broader cultural and individual belief systems. By the nineteenth century, the Tarot had become a treasury of occult wisdom, and yet the earliest Tarot deck simply commemorated a medieval wedding. So what happened in the intervening centuries to change Tarot from courtly art form to high magic?

It is thought that Tarot cards were originally designed for sole use at the royal courts of Europe, for games and divination. In 1392, a painter named Jacquemin Grigonneur was commissioned to paint three packs of richly decorated cards, "ornamented with many devices," for Charles VI of France. His fee was entered into the court treasurer's ledger, which is

ABOVE: *Justice from the Charles VI (Grigonneur) deck of 1392, although it is more likely that these cards are of fifteenth-century origin. The red-haired female figure appears prominently on Justice, Strength, and Temperance.*

ABOVE: *The High Priestess, or Papess, of the Visconti-Sforza deck. The Visconti family had her painted in the likeness of their ancestor, Sister Manfreda, who was a member of a religious sect who had elected her as Papess. She was burned at the stake for heresy.*

considered the first documented evidence of specific decks of Tarot cards in Europe. Seventeen cards supposedly from this deck, and known as the Grigonneur or Charles VI deck, are preserved at the Bibliothèque Nationale, Paris. However, it is unlikely that these cards are the Grigonneur ones—some scholars believe that they are Venetian and were painted in the mid-fifteenth century. The clue to this lies in the style of armor worn by the Page of Swords, which is of a later design more consistent with the fifteenth than fourteenth century.

Italian courts were commissioning their own Tarot cards as early as 1415, when a deck—the Visconti Tarot—was painted for the Duke of Milan, probably by the artist Bonifacio Bembo. Its successor, the Visconti-Sforza Tarot (see page 155) is the oldest Tarot still in existence. Over 550 years old, it remains in use today.

The Visconti-Sforza Tarot is thought to have been created to commemorate the marriage of Bianca-Maria Visconti to Francesco Sforza in 1441. The marriage represented the alliance of two of the most powerful families in northern Italy, and reflects the earliest tradition of exquisite, hand-painted cards, which often carried the family insignia. The Ace of Staves (Wands) of the Visconti-Sforza Tarot is inscribed with the motto "A bon droyt"—which is variously translated as "with good reason" or "the right path." The seventy-eight-card pack expresses the structure and imagery of many modern decks. In Italy, the term Venetian or Piedmontese is used to refer to all decks of seventy-eight cards, as opposed to decks such as the ninety-seven-card Florentine pack (known as a *minchiate*) and the Bolognese pack, which comprises sixty-two cards.

RIGHT: *Hand-painted Italian Tarot card, possibly fifteenth century. A young man with a crossbow is depicted with an emblem of a wand, indicating that he may be the Page of Wands, or Batons.*

Tarot as Trade

The invention of woodblock printing in Germany in the early 1400s marked the beginning of mass production and the rise in popularity of playing cards and Tarot cards among ordinary people. By the mid-1400s, card-making workshops were flourishing in Italy, France, Germany, and Belgium, and card-painting soon became a specialized trade acknowledged by craftsmen's guilds. Religious opposition to Tarot cards, and the banning of foreign imports (whether playing cards or Tarot decks), reveals their prevalence, popularity, and economic viability at this time. In the mid-fifteenth century a Franciscan friar preached a sermon in northern Italy condemning dice and Tarot cards, and the Church referred to Tarot cards as "the devil's picture book," which may have been part of a general plan to suppress the philosophy of Gnosticism throughout Europe. Gnostics (from the Greek word *gnosis*, meaning "knowledge") believed in esoteric wisdom, which the Church deemed heretic.

ABOVE: *In woodblock printing, the outlines of the card images were printed, and then the colors were stenciled or hand-painted. The Marseilles deck is an example of this production method; its design was based on earlier Tarot styles. The Tarot of Marseilles was published in 1701–15 by the artist Jean Dodal. Later decks were painted by Nicolas Conver, master papermaker at Marseilles in 1761.*

Where Did The Name Tarot Come From?

ABOVE: *The Crocodile, or Fool, from the Grand Tarot Belline, a nineteenth-century French deck conceived by one psychic, Magus Edmond, and published by another, Magus Belline. The card's interpretation may roughly translate as: "All kinds of misfortune threaten you. There is nothing to fear, as you only have to wait for salvation from heaven."*

The multitude of theories about the origin of the word Tarot reflects the debate surrounding the true origin of the cards themselves. There is little factual evidence to support any of these claims—only the interpretations of Tarot historians and occultists.

The simplest explanation is that the word Tarot is a diminutive of *tarocchi*, the Italian card game from which the Tarot developed. Alternatively, the cards may have been named after the River Taro in the plains of northern Italy, where the oldest surviving deck, the Visconti-Sforza, was painted.

Occultists of the 1700s and 1800s, a time of esoteric revival in Europe, assign an Egyptian connection: "Tarot" stems from the Egyptian word *Ta-rosh*, meaning "the royal way," associating the cards with the pharaohs as both earthly and divine kings; however, this meaning also links to the Tarot's emergence in Europe as a practice of the royal courts. The word may also be a version of Thoth, who was the Egyptian god of healing, wisdom, and the occult. "Taro" could equally be an anagram of the Latin word *rota*, meaning "a wheel," because the sequence of cards symbolizes the circle of life from birth to death. It could also come from *Torah*, Hebrew for "the law," thereby aligning the Tarot with kabbala, the Judaic mystical system.

Some theorists believe that the Tarot developed in the Orient, named after the village of Tarot in Myanmar (Burma), or after Lake Tarok Tso in southwest Tibet. However, it is more likely that the minor arcana, or numbered playing cards, originated in the Orient (see page 14).

Knights and Gypsies

ABOVE: *The Knight of Wands from the IJJ Swiss Tarot is dressed cavalier-style, his red tunic symbolizing the energy of the suit.*

Some people believe that the Roma (Romanies), or "gypsies," brought Tarot cards to Europe. The word "gypsy" is a corruption of "Egyptian," derived from Little Egypt (Epirus), a region of Peloponnesia in Greece. However, it is believed that the Roma originally came from India. There is no real evidence that they invented the Tarot; it is more likely that they adopted and popularized the cards throughout Europe as they emigrated west during the 1400s. The idea of the Tarot was already familiar to some medieval Europeans before the 1400s: in a sermon in Switzerland in 1377, the German monk Brother Johannes von Rheinfelden, of Bredfield monastery, described a series of painted cards that worked as a pictorial allegory of life and the journey of the soul. This suggests that he was referring to the Tarot and the symbolism of the major arcana cards.

Gnostic sects in Europe may have used Tarot cards to teach the illiterate their belief in Dualism, which is the interplay of opposites. These opposites—male and female, darkness and light, death and rebirth—are common themes in the Tarot. In this way, Tarot themes and archetypes were perhaps used for instructional rather than divinatory purposes. The Waldenses, a Christian dissident sect founded by Peter Waldo in 1170, may have used the cards as a secret code. The sect was banned by the Church, but thrived in secret, so Waldensian missionaries traveled throughout Italy (often in disguise) seeking converts. Known as *barbe*, or

uncles, they would dress as tradesmen to ensure their safe passage. The Magician card may have represented a *barb* in disguise, since in early decks the Magician is shown as a cobbler. Roger Tilley, in his book *The History of Playing Cards*, proposes that the Magician card may have been used by Waldensians as a passport to identify themselves to other devotees.

The Knights Templar, an ascetic military order, was also attributed with the distribution of Tarot cards. The order was founded by Hugh de Payens of Burgundy and Godeffroi de St Omer, a French knight, in 1119. Their mission was to protect pilgrims and the routes to the Holy Land. Over time, the order became rich and successful. As its influence grew, the Knights became a target for persecution by the Church, which sought to stamp out the many unorthodox sects operating at the time. Philip IV of France charged the Knights with heresy; they were arrested and their possessions seized. Their grand master, Jacques de Molay, was burned at the stake in 1314. Again, there is no documented evidence to tie the Knights Templar in with the Tarot—however, a cross appearing on the Ace of Coins cards in the French Vieville pack has been identified as the Templars' insignia.

ABOVE: *The Knight of Cups from the Visconti-Sforza deck. A graceful youth on horseback holds the chalice, his suit symbol. His offering of emotion may be at odds with the more forceful energy generally associated with the knights.*

ABOVE: *The Knight of Swords from the Tarot of Marseilles. The Knights denote action and in Tarot are indicators of events speeding up. The knight is the only court card not to make it into a modern deck of playing cards.*

The Origins of the Minor Arcana

ABOVE: *The Ace of Swords, shown with a crown and decorative fronds, is from the Liguria Piedmont Tarot, published in 1860. The style of this deck shows the fusion of both Italian and French Tarot traditions.*

BECAUSE THE TAROT IS MADE UP of twenty-two major arcana cards, or trumps (triumphs), and fifty-six minor arcana cards, which are divided into four suits, it is likely that these arcanas may have existed separately and were combined to form the complete seventy-eight-card deck at a later stage. The minor arcana originated from playing cards thought to have come from eleventh-century China and Korea, where sets with four suits were in use at court. Early decks from southern China often have the suits Coins, Strings of Coins, Myriads of Strings, and Tens of Myriads—the forerunners of Hearts, Spades, Clubs, and Diamonds of our modern playing cards. In medieval Italy, merchants plied the trade routes from Venice to the Orient, so it is quite likely that the card-painters of northern Italy were exposed to, and influenced by, Oriental card systems.

The Italian author Giovanni di Covelluzzo, writing in 1480, had yet another theory, but little evidence. He believed that playing cards were introduced into Italy in 1379 from Arabic North Africa. If this happened at all, it is more likely that the minor arcana reached Italy from North Africa via Spain, which was Arab-occupied until 1492. In Spain, these cards are known as *naipes;* when they appeared in Italy, they were known by their Saracen name, *naib.*

ABOVE: *The Ace of Cups, probably dating from fifteenth-century Italy, shows a central chalice with a double-arced fountain. An arrow appears where the two streams of water divide, and a sword is depicted to the right.*

THE LEGEND OF THE GRAIL

The legend of the Holy Grail provides another mysterious link to the possible origin of the minor arcana cards. The Four Grail Hallows were the grail itself, or the chalice used by Christ at the Last Supper; the sword used by King David in the Old Testament; the sacred lance that pierced Christ's side during his crucifixion; and the platter that held the Passover lamb.

Perhaps the best-known example of the grail stories in medieval England is *Morte D'Arthur*, a compilation of grail legends written by the English knight Sir Thomas Malory. Published in 1485, it is likely that Malory's work was based partly on the earlier work of Chrétien de Troyes in the late 1100s. De Troyes, a French writer, penned Arthurian romances for his many wealthy patrons to satisfy their curiosity about British mythology after the Norman Conquest. He, in turn, was inspired by Celtic mythology.

The Irish predecessors of the Four Grail Hallows were the Four Treasures of Ireland: the Cauldron of the Dagda, the Spear of Lug, the Sword of Nuada, and the Stone of Fa. Many contemporary Tarot packs draw on these legends and name their minor arcana suits after the treasures. The Cauldron equates to Cups, the Spear of Lug to Wands, the Sword of Nuada to Swords, and the Stone of Fa to Pentacles. The Arthurian Tarot uses the characters and sacred objects of the grail legend in its major arcana. Card I, the Magician, is Merlin; the High Priestess is the Lady of the Lake; the Emperor is King Arthur; and the Wheel of Fortune is the Round Table.

THE FOUR SUITS OF VISHNU

The Hindu creator-god, Vishnu, is another source of answers to the Tarot mystery. The four suits of the minor arcana may be symbolized by his four arms, in which he holds four sacred objects, some of which correspond directly to the emblems of the suits. He holds the disk, for preservation (Pentacles); and the club, for wisdom (Wands). The third object is the lotus, for love; associated with femininity, the lotus may link with the suit of Cups. The conch, for inner realization, does not at first glance sit well with the remaining suit of Swords. However, in Hindu tradition the conch was used to sound the war-cry before battle, so it does imply the martial nature of Swords after all.

The Occult Revival: Egyptomania

ABOVE: *This modern Egyptian Tarot, painted on papyrus by Silvana Alasia, was partly influenced by the Tarot created by the late nineteenth-century occultist Jean-Baptiste Pitois, a follower of Eliphas Levi (see page 17).*

THE LATE EIGHTEENTH and early nineteenth century saw an occult revival. Many of the associations made with the Tarot at this time have influenced modern thinking on the card meanings. Up to this point, there had been no obvious link between the Tarot and Egypt or kabbala.

The landmark text of the occult revival was authored by French esotericist Antoine Court de Gebelin. In his treatise *Monde primitif* of 1781, de Gebelin claimed that the Tarot itself was actually an ancient Egyptian book containing secret wisdom. This was the Book of Thoth, named after the Egyptian god of healing, wisdom, and the occult.

After de Gebelin's death in 1784, a Parisian barber and wigmaker (or merchant, according to some sources) Jean-Baptiste Alliette, continued his work. Under the chosen name Etteilla—Alliette spelled backward—he wrote esoteric books, worked as a fortune teller, and produced his own Etteilla Tarot deck. He claimed that in this deck he had restored the ancient Egyptian designs. He also included the Tarot's links with kabbala, the mystical tradition that originated in Judaism (see page 24). When Napoleon invaded Egypt in 1798, Egyptomania reigned; as artifacts raided from tombs and temples found their way to Europe, the work of de Gebelin and Etteilla gained credence and popularity.

ABOVE: *The Moon from The Tarot of the Sphinx*, by Silvana Alasia. In this modern deck, two Anubis dogs replace the traditional dogs or wolves, and pyramids symbolize the two towers that define the perimeter of the moonlit landscape.

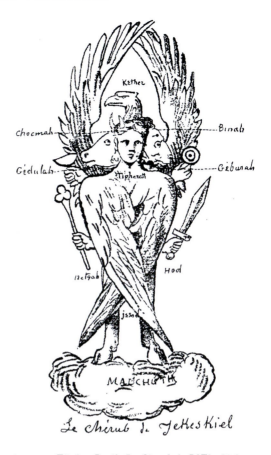

ABOVE: *Eliphas Levi's Le Cherub de L'Ekeskiel (Cherub of Ezekiel), from his work* Dogme et Rituel de la Haute Magie, *1854.*

The story continues with the prominent occultist Alphonse Louis Constant, who went by his chosen name of Eliphas Levi. In the mid-1800s, this French Rosicrucian developed the possible link between the major arcana and kabbala by explaining how the twenty-two letters of the Hebrew alphabet corresponded to the twenty-two major arcana cards of the Tarot (see page 62). Levi's illustration, *Le Cherub de L'Ekeskiel* (see top right), shows how he combined kabbala with the Tarot. He drew a cherub based on the vision of Ezekiel, as described in Genesis in the Old Testament—this is a traditional cherub, rather than the familiar *pucci*, or chubby winged infant, that we generally envisage. Levi's sketch shows the four holy living creatures of Ezekiel's vision: the cherub itself, the eagle, lion, and bull. But he added four hands, each of which holds an emblem of the four suits of the minor arcana: the sword, wand, pentacle, and cup. He also annotated his work with the names of the ten sephira (energy centers) of the kabbala: kether, chokmah, binah, chesed, geburah, tipereth, netzach, hod, yesod, and malkuth (see page 25). Many Tarot decks, such as the Rider Waite, show card XXI, the World, with the four living creatures surrounding the garlanded dancer.

MYSTICAL ORDERS

The Hermetic Order of the Golden Dawn, a British occult society, created a system of magic that wove together the kabbalistic, astrological, and Egyptian Tarot associations. It was founded in 1888, during the occult revival, by William Wynn Westcott and William Robert Woodman, both doctors, and Samuel Liddell Mathers (later MacGregor Mathers). All three were masons. The "order" of the Golden Dawn was based on a hierarchy of ten degrees, from the ten sephira of kabbala (see page 25). It devised a list of Tarot associations that is nowadays the one most generally accepted; it presented the element, the planetary influence, Tree of Life pathway, and Hebrew letter for each major arcana card.

ABOVE: *The Chariot, Oswald Wirth Tarot. The Egyptian and kabbalistic influence is evident in the Wirth Tarot. The chariot is pulled by two sphinxes, and the chariot itself is adorned by the winged sun disc of Egypt. The Hebrew letter vav appears on the lower right corner of the card.*

The order also developed the divinatory meanings of the minor arcana cards, and presented fully illustrated numbered (or "pip") cards, rather than showing a simple geometric design. One leading light of the order was Arthur Edward Waite, the originator of the Rider Waite Tarot deck. Waite's deck, illustrated by Pamela Colman Smith, was published in 1910 before the eventual demise of the order in 1914. The Rider Waite deck is based on the card meanings of the Order of the Golden Dawn, and is still one of the most popular decks in use today.

The infamous magician Aleister Crowley was initiated into the order in 1889, yet his Tarot cards—known as the Book of Thoth, or Thoth deck—did not appear until

1944, three years before his death. The limited-edition cards were illustrated by Lady Frieda Harris and only became available to the general public much later, in 1969. Crowley, "an unspeakable mad person" according to fellow initiate W. B. Yeats, left the order in 1900 after a disagreement with MacGregor Mathers. By 1907, however, he had founded the Argentinum Astrum, or Order of the Silver Star. This was his own magical society, whose key text, *The Book of the Law*, had been channeled by Crowley himself, posing as the Prince Chioa Kahn at the Great Pyramid of Egypt. Crowley's cult combined his interest in sexual magic with some of the rituals taken from the Golden Dawn.

ABOVE: *The Lovers from the Rider Waite Tarot, illustrated by Pamela Colman Smith and directed by A. E. Waite. The artist's insigna appears on the lower right side of the card, by the leg of the male lover.*

ABOVE: *Judgment, by American artist Beth Moon, 2002. Moon's work is inspired by the mythical and spiritual aspects of Tarot as a path of spiritual ascension.*
It is increasingly common to see innovative art and design in modern decks. Tarots may be illustrated with photographic images or photo-montages, providing a new view of an age-old subject.

The Golden Dawn tradition continues today. The American occultist Paul Foster Case, who was born in 1884, was so influenced by the order and by Waite's landmark deck that he founded his own order, the Builders of the Adytum (BOTA). BOTA is an international Tarot organization based in Los Angeles. It has its own black-and-white Tarot cards, illustrated by Jesse Burns Parke, which are based on the Rider Waite designs. Tarot students color in the cards, following a precise code.

2 TAROT SYMBOLISM
Using Astrology with the Tarot

The astrological associations generally used in Tarot are those devised by the Hermetic Order of the Golden Dawn (see page 18). However, their original pairings of cards with the planets, zodiacal signs, and elements was based on the seven known planets that could be seen from the Earth: the Sun, Moon, Mercury, Venus, Mars, Jupiter, and Saturn. The distant planet Uranus had been discovered in 1781 (the first planet to be identified using a telescope), followed by Neptune in 1846; Pluto was not identified until 1930, after the order had officially ended. Below is a rectified list that includes all ten planets, plus the twelve astrological signs. Note that only three out of the four elements appear—Air (the Fool), Water (the Hanged Man), and Fire (Judgment). It is possible to use the dates of the zodiac signs to time your readings (see page 22).

LEFT: *The Ace of Coins from the Minchiate Florentine, a sixteenth-century Italian deck (see also the caption, page 21). The card shown here is a reproduction of the original deck of 1725, which consists of ninety-seven cards. The additional cards are: the three theological virtues, Faith, Hope, and Charity (see also page 83); one cardinal virtue, Prudence; the four elements; and the twelve zodiac signs. The Pope is not included in this minchiate deck.*

TAROT SYMBOLISM

ABOVE: *The Emperor from the Minchiate Florentine, 1725. This deck incorporates the traditional virtues and allegories of the era with the signs of the zodiac. In some Tarots the Emperor is associated with Aries (see right); in others, with Jupiter.*

Common Planetary Associations of The Major Arcana

0 THE FOOL	AIR, URANUS
I THE MAGICIAN	MERCURY
II THE HIGH PRIESTESS	THE MOON
III THE EMPRESS	VENUS
IV THE EMPEROR	ARIES
V THE HIEROPHANT	TAURUS
VI THE LOVERS	GEMINI
VII THE CHARIOT	CANCER
VIII JUSTICE	LIBRA
IX THE HERMIT	VIRGO
X THE WHEEL OF FORTUNE	JUPITER
XI STRENGTH	LEO
XII THE HANGED MAN	WATER, NEPTUNE
XIII DEATH	SCORPIO
XIV TEMPERANCE	SAGITTARIUS
XV THE DEVIL	CAPRICORN
XVI THE TOWER	MARS
XVII THE STAR	AQUARIUS
XVIII THE MOON	PISCES
XIX THE SUN	THE SUN
XX JUDGMENT	FIRE, PLUTO
XXI THE WORLD	SATURN

The Elements and The Minor Arcana

The four elements are mirrors of nature itself and of the nature of human beings. Earth, Fire, Water, and Air are vital for life, and they are designed to support each other to maintain equilibrium: without Air, Fire will die; without Water, Earth cannot survive.

The four suits of the minor arcana are associated with the four elements of Earth, Fire, Water, and Air. The system of elements and their relationship to distinct energies, or personality types, dates to the fourth century BCE and Aristotle's theory on the ratio of opposites. Fire was associated with warmth, Earth was dry, Air cool, and Water moist. Even from these basic descriptions, we can see implicit character traits: cool-headed, intelligent Air signs reveal the nature of the logical Swords; receptive Water signs link with emotional Cups. This thinking can also be seen in twentieth-century psychology. Carl Jung saw the "four basic functions" of our nature as thinking, sensation, intuition, and feeling. Relating this to the elements and minor arcana suits, we get Swords/Air as

THE MYSTERY OF THE TAROT

"thinking," Pentacles/Earth as "sensation," Wands/Fire as "intuition," and Cups/Water as "feeling." A simple interpretation of this theory, shown below, can act as an *aide-memoire* in a reading:

SWORDS/AIR: *I THINK*   WANDS/FIRE: *I WANT*
PENTACLES/EARTH: *I HAVE*   CUPS/WATER: *I FEEL*.

In astrology, each element relates to the three signs of the zodiac that share that element. For example, Water suggests the water signs of Cancer, Scorpio, and Pisces. This system can be helpful when trying to identify a Court card, for example. The Queen of Cups will therefore be a woman born under Cancer, Scorpio, or Pisces.

CUPS: WATER
The signs of Cancer, Scorpio, and Pisces

WANDS: FIRE

The signs of Aries, Leo, and Sagittarius

PENTACLES: EARTH
The signs of Virgo, Taurus, and Capricorn

SWORDS: AIR

The signs of Gemini, Libra, and Aquarius

USING ASTROLOGY TO TIME YOUR READINGS

The four elements traditionally relate to the four seasons—Air (Sword) cards are winter; Water (Cups) cards are summer; Fire (Wands) cards are spring; and Earth (Pentacles) cards relate to fall. With the major arcana (as shown in the charts on pages 21 and 23), some of the major trumps relate to specific zodiac signs. You can use the dates for each star sign as a way to time a reading. For example, the Hermit relates to Virgo, so the influence of this card may occur between August 24 and September 23. The influence of the Devil is linked to the time of Capricorn, between December 22 and January 20; interestingly, this relates to the Christmas and New Year period, when we are tempted to overindulge. On page 23 is a list of the major arcana cards that relate to signs of the zodiac and their respective dates. For specific spreads that you can use to time your readings, see pages 53–60.

TAROT SYMBOLISM

THE EMPEROR	ARIES	MARCH 21–APRIL 20
THE HIEROPHANT	TAURUS	APRIL 21–MAY 21
THE LOVERS	GEMINI	MAY 22–JUNE 21
THE CHARIOT	CANCER	JUNE 22–JULY 23
STRENGTH	LEO	JULY 24–AUGUST 23
THE HERMIT	VIRGO	AUGUST 24–SEPTEMBER 23
JUSTICE	LIBRA	SEPTEMBER 24–OCTOBER 23
DEATH	SCORPIO	OCTOBER 24–NOVEMBER 22
TEMPERANCE	SAGITTARIUS	NOVEMBER 23–DECEMBER 21
THE DEVIL	CAPRICORN	DECEMBER 22–JANUARY 20
THE STAR	AQUARIUS	JANUARY 21–FEBRUARY 19
THE MOON	PISCES	FEBRUARY 20–MARCH 20

ABOVE: *The Sun, The Moon, and The Star, from the Visconti-Sforza deck. These three cards are the cosmic cards of the Tarot. A lone female figure or a cherub hold aloft the symbol for their card, perhaps collectively signifying the potential and challenge of human spirituality.*

The Tarot and Kabbala

ABOVE: *The Fool, Etteilla Spanish Tarot, late nineteenth century. This deck includes the upright and reversed card meanings with their Hebrew letters. The letter hei appears on the Fool, so it is unlikely that the card artist followed the systems of Papus, Eliphas Levi or MacGregor Mathers (see page 26), who linked the Fool with the letter aleph.*

KABBALA IS THE MYSTICAL BELIEF SYSTEM derived from Judaism. Many Tarot readers use the correspondences between kabbala's Tree of Life, its central symbol, and the Tarot to divine deeper meanings from the cards. The emergence of kabbala can be linked to the *Sefer Yetzirah*, or Book of Creation. There is no exact date for its origin or distribution, but it is thought that it was written between the third and sixth centuries CE. It includes meditations that were based on the twenty-two letters of the Hebrew alphabet.

The late 1400s saw the publication of a kabbalistic classic: the *Zohar*, or Book of Splendor. Its author was supposedly the second-century rabbi Shimon ben Yohai, although Spanish kabbalist Moses De Leon, who claimed to have discovered the book, was also rumored to have written it. The *Zohar* is a commentary on the Torah, written in Aramaic. It had a significant impact on the development of kabbala as a mystical system.

The *Zohar* revealed the Tree of Life, which showed twenty-two pathways connecting the ten sephira (vortexes of energy) through which God created the world. The purpose of the tree is to show the nature of the relationships between people and the universe by means of connective pathways. The tree can also be seen as three pillars: the left side is associated with femininity and judgment; the right side with masculinity and mercy; the sephira in the central column are concerned with equilibrium, for here all the qualities of the left and right sephira must be synthesized to create wholeness and integral wisdom.

Kabbalists linked each major arcana card with one of the twenty-two pathways on the tree. By understanding the energies of the pathway and their connecting sephira, we can understand the deeper qualities of the card. The Devil, for example, links the two sephira of tipereth (meaning harmony) and hod (power and glory). This may be the temptation expressed by the card when one is caught between wanting to feel powerful and choosing a path of peace. Different sources assign slightly different meanings to the sephira, but the most widely used interpretations are given in the list below.

ABOVE: *The Tower, Etteilla Spanish Tarot, late nineteenth century. Etteilla, a French occultist and Tarot-card reader (see page 16), influenced the esoteric development of the Tarot.*
BELOW: *The Hebrew letters tzaddi (right); pei (centre); beit (left).*

KEY TO THE SEPHIRA (SEE ILLUSTRATION OVERLEAF)

1 KETHER: CROWN, UNITY, PERFECTION
2 CHOKMAH: WISDOM, INTUITION
3 BINAH: UNDERSTANDING, EXPERIENCE
4 CHESED: LOVE
5 GEBURAH: JUDGMENT
6 TIPERETH: HARMONY, BEAUTY
7 NETZACH: VICTORY, STRENGTH
8 HOD: GLORY, POWER
9 YESOD: FOUNDATION, UNCONSCIOUS
10 MALKUTH: KINGDOM, REAL EXISTENCE

THE MYSTERY OF THE TAROT

LEFT: *The Tree of Life Tarot, 1983, is designed as a spiritual mirror more than a divining tool. Each major arcana card shows the Tree of Life with its associated sephirot. See the previous page for the key to the sephira.*

KABBALA AND THE MAJOR ARCANA

There are three versions of the correspondences between the Tarot trumps and the Hebrew alphabet: those of Eliphas Levi (see page 17), the Spanish-born occultist Papus (Dr. Gerald Encausse), and MacGregor Mathers, a key member of the Order of the Golden Dawn (see page 18). The chart below is organized according to Mathers' system, which begins with card 0, the Fool.

MAJOR ARCANA CORRESPONDENCES WITH THE HEBREW ALPHABET

CARD	HEBREW LETTER	COMMON MEANING
0 THE FOOL	ALEPH	INSTINCT
I THE MAGICIAN	BEIT	CREATIVITY
II THE HIGH PRIESTESS	GIMEL	WISDOM
III THE EMPRESS	DALED	ATTAINMENT
IV THE EMPEROR	HEI	ADVANCEMENT
V THE HIEROPHANT	VAV	KINDNESS
VI THE LOVERS	ZAYIN	SOULFULNESS
VII THE CHARIOT	CHET	GUIDANCE
VIII *STRENGTH	TET	COURAGE
IX THE HERMIT	YOD	PRUDENCE
X THE WHEEL OF FORTUNE	KAPH	DESTINY
XI *JUSTICE	LAMED	FAIRNESS

XII The Hanged Man	Mem	Transition
XIII Death	Nun	Decline; rebirth
XIV Temperance	Samekh	Patience
XV Devil	Ayin	Clear vision
XVI The Tower	Pei	Chaos
XVII The Star	Tzaddi	Hope
XVIII The Moon	Kuf	Hidden problems
XIX The Sun	Resh	Success
XX Judgment	Shin	Renewal
XXI The World	Tav	Completion

* Note that the position of Strength and Justice is reversed in the Golden Dawn system.

Kabbala and The Minor Arcana

Eliphas Levi established a link between the four suits of the minor arcana and the Tetragrammaton, or four Hebrew letters, that represent the Yahweh or Jehovah, the name of God: YHVH (Y = suit of Wands, H = Cups, V = Swords, H = Pentacles). The numbered minor arcana cards are linked with their associated numbered sephira, as shown below.

Sephirot Number and Name   Minor Arcana Card

1 Kether: Unity, perfection	Aces
2 Chokmah: Wisdom, intuition	Twos
3 Binah: Understanding	Threes
4 Chesed: Love	Fours
5 Geburah: Judgment	Fives
6 Tipereth: Harmony, beauty	Sixes
7 Netzach: Victory, strength	Sevens
8 Hod: Glory, power	Eights
9 Yesod: The unconscious	Nines
10 Malkuth: Real existence	Tens

ABOVE: *The Aleph, or Fool, card from a modern Tarot kabbala deck. The letter aleph appears at the lower corners.*

LEFT: *Hebrew letters tet (right); kuf, or kaph (left).*

The Tarot Menagerie

The Tarot speaks in the language of symbols,
the language of the unconscious, and when approached in the right
manner it may open a door into the hidden
reaches of the soul.

ALFRED DOUGLAS, *The Tarot*

IN THE CARDS OF THE MAJOR ARCANA, animals appear as symbols of our deepest instincts. They act as messengers or reminders of our mortality, of the fluctuating cycles of birth, death, and rebirth over which we have little control. The animals of the Tarot range from the domestic dog of the Fool to the mythic dragon of the Wheel of Fortune, and from the snake of the Hermit to the wolves of the Moon. Understanding their significance in the Tarot can be allied to interpreting animals in our dreams, because they too help us access important information from the unconscious.

THE SNAKE: INSTINCT

The snake appears on card IX, entwined around the staff of the Hermit. As earth-dwellers, snakes are perceived in many cultures as symbols of fertility. In Greek mythology, serpents or dragons were said to pull the chariot of the earth goddess Demeter. In Hindu myth, however, snakes appear as evil *nagas*, and in Christianity as an agent of corruption in the Garden of Eden. Yet the Hermit's snake is not out of control: the tamed snake symbolizes his instinctive wisdom and a fertile mind that will guide him through the underworld of the unconscious.

The Crayfish: The Soul

On card XVIII, the Moon, a crayfish or lobster is part submerged in water, while its upper body makes a primitive cry toward the light of the moon. In mythology, fish represent the soul, our deepest level of instinct. In the Fenian cycle of Irish legends, the warrior hero, Finn, eats a magical salmon that gives him knowledge of all things. Early Christians used the fish as a secret sign of their faith, which links to the meaning of the card as a whole: a crisis of faith.

The Horse: Conflict and Passion

Horses appear throughout the minor arcana on all the Knight cards. This indicates that they are essentially the action men of the Court cards, speeding up events and signaling change and possibly adventure. In the major arcana, horses appear on card VII, the Chariot. The charioteer is successful through the force of his personality, carefully harnessing life's conflicts and obstacles, which are symbolized by the white and dark horses. In psychological terms, the harnessed horses symbolize libido under control.

The Lion: Strength

A symbol of sovereignty, the lion is often associated with supreme power, strength, and even destruction. The Egyptian lion-headed goddess, Sekhmet, was sent by the sun god to annihilate a human rebellion; in Greek mythology, Herakles's first labor was to kill the terrifying lion of Nemea. In card XI, Strength, a man or woman passively restrains the jaws of the lion, taming the primitive through gentleness rather than force. The symbol of the lion alongside the figure of civility, or higher self, shows the reconciliation of opposite aspects of human nature.

The Dragon: Primal Power

The dragon appears on many Wheel of Fortune cards, as a miniature figure of Justice brandishing a sword with which he judges the soul of humans and guards the underworld. The dragon symbolizes the primal energy of nature.

The Monkey: Vanity

The monkey represents vanity and impermanence. He is often shown clambering on the side of the Wheel of Fortune, or grinding the wheel itself, as the other beasts or people rise and fall at his will.

The Ass: Folly

The ass or donkey is a traditional symbol of folly, but also represents submission. Christ chose this lowliest of animals to carry him into Jerusalem as a symbol of humility. On the Wheel of Fortune, the ass is often shown clinging to the wheel itself, powerless against the force of the turning world.

The Dog: Conscience

The dog appears on the Fool card, pawing at his distracted master, like a bad attack of his conscience. As with all animals in the Tarot, the dog represents primitive urges—here, a natural desire to protect another from danger—that is inherent for our survival.

The Tarot Rainbow

COLORS ARE OFTEN USED IN THE TAROT AS A CODE. In decks such as the Marseilles, some Tarot scholars have deconstructed the use of color and assigned particular significance to those used. However, as with all art forms, practicality is an important factor. The four or five basic colors used on the original Marseilles deck would have reflected what was available to the printers at the time, or what was economically viable for the card makers to use. In the early hand-painted decks made for kings and dukes, expensive colors may have been more feasible.

It is important to refer to your own particular deck when interpreting colors, as some have their own color systems. The Sacred Rose deck, for example, uses five colors of a rose as its color code: the red rose for sacrifice, white for purity, blue for impossibility, gold for absolute achievement, and purple for time and space. Below is a list of common colors and associations that you can use as an aid to interpretation.

Red

Creativity, vitality, and strength. The Magician traditionally wears a red robe to suggest his energy. Some Tarot decks use red as a theme for the Swords cards, due to its association with the blood of conflict.

Yellow

The intellect, logic, and self-expression. Some Tarot decks use yellow as a theme for the Swords, or for Pentacles, because yellow is associated with Earth, the element of the latter suit.

Blue

Spirituality, intuition, and truth, hence "true blue." The High Priestess often wears blue like Isis, the Egyptian madonna (see page 73). Some Tarots use blue as a theme for Cups, to signify its element, emotional Water. In Temperance (left) blue also symbolizes water, which here must be carefully controlled.

Green

Nature, fertility, and protection. In the Visconti-Sforza deck, the Empress has green hands, to show her fertility. Some Tarot decks use green as a theme for the suit of Wands.

Naturals

Natural colors such as beige, cream, and flesh tones denote material issues and, for some cards, sacrifice. In the Visconti-Sforza Tarot deck, the High Priestess wears a pale wool habit rather than the traditional blue (see above) as a sign of humility; the half-clothed, impoverished Fool is a symbol of the self-sacrifice of Lent.

White

White symbolizes purity, perfection, and innocence. The Rider Waite Tarot card for the Sun shows a child riding a white horse, which denotes innocence.

3 HOW TO LAY THE CARDS
THE TAROT READINGS

Choosing a Deck

IT IS IMPORTANT TO CHOOSE A DECK that you really like. You will have it for a long time and you have to live with it; people rarely give away their cards, so unless you inherit an unwanted Tarot deck, you will need to purchase your own. There are so-called traditions that dictate that you should not buy your own cards, but that they should be bought for you as a gift. Do not worry about this—choosing cards is such a personal experience that it would be difficult to rely on someone else to do this for you.

If you have not bought a Tarot deck before, try a twentieth-century one that has illustrated "pip" or numbered cards, such as the Rider Waite deck. The images on the card will stir your memory if you already have some familiarity with the Tarot, or will help you learn the card meanings from scratch. If you choose a deck with geometric suit designs for the numbered cards, buy an additional guidebook (such as this one)—you may want more in-depth information than you will obtain from the instruction leaflet inside the box.

Always treat your Tarot cards with respect. Keep them wrapped in a dark cloth, preferably in a box or drawer. They are personal to you, so do not leave them on display for others to touch. It is important that they absorb your energy as you continually handle them. This is why some Tarotists recommend sleeping with a new deck under your pillow for the first few weeks after purchase.

Shown opposite is a list of well-known decks and their country of origin or style. This is a very small selection and is not intended to be comprehensive. To investigate the hundreds of available decks, see page 155 for a list of Tarot resources.

ABOVE: *The Queen of Pentacles from the Tarot of Marseilles. The Marseilles is one of the most influential decks in the history of Tarot (see pages 10, 13, 33).*

France

TAROT OF MARSEILLES (1761) Painted by artist Nicolas Conver, master papermaker at Marseilles. A classic, popular deck; the forerunner of modern playing-card designs.

Germany

ZIGEUNER TAROT (1975) Designed by Walter Wegmuller. Richly illustrated in a modern style, these popular cards show Hebrew letters and the traditional Arabic numerals.

Italy

VISCONTI-SFORZA TAROTS Reproductions of fifteenth-century Tarot decks (see pages 9, 13, 23, 64, 155).

Japan

UKIYOE TAROT (1982) Art-directed by Stuart R. Kaplan and painted by Koji Furuta in the style of the *ukiyo-e* art tradition, which flourished in Japan during the mid-seventeenth century.

ABOVE: *The Star from the Crystal Tarot illustrated by Elisabetta Trevisan.*

Switzerland

IJJ SWISS TAROT A traditional late eighteenth- to early nineteenth-century pack, in which the Pope (Hierophant) and the Papess (High Priestess) are replaced by the gods Jupiter and Juno, giving the pack its JJ moniker.

United Kingdom

RIDER WAITE TAROT (1910) Illustrated by Pamela Colman Smith, directed by A. E. Waite, a leading member of the Hermetic Order of the Golden Dawn (see page 18). The first deck to have pictorial "pip" cards.

United States

SACRED ROSE TAROT (1982) Illustrated by Johanna Sherman and inspired by the sacred lotus of the Orient. The "pip" cards are fully illustrated.

ABOVE: *The Zigeuner Tarot (1975) by gypsy artist Walter Wegmuller.*

MYTHIC TAROT (1986) Written and art-directed by Juliet Sharman-Burke and Liz Greene, and illustrated by Tricia Newell. A fully illustrated Tarot based on Greek mythology.

When to Read the Cards

When reading for yourself, make it a habit to read when you feel that you don't need to. This may sound contrary to the traditional view of needing a reading because you have decisions to make, or other pressing events about which you seek clarity. However, reading the cards when you don't have an urgent question can help you develop a more detached attitude; the greatest difficulty when using the Tarot for yourself for prediction is having an agenda before you begin. When you interpret your own cards, it is tempting to see what you want to see. If you are a beginner, try reading for yourself alongside a friend, and ask them what they think as you interpret. This does not diminish your reading. Consulting the cards is what you make of it: the card's archetypes act to stimulate your memory and subconscious. They only have the power that you give them.

Start by reading for yourself once a week. Keep a Tarot diary, and note the cards that come up each time. Vary the spreads that you use—start with a three-card spread and progress to more complex arrangements as you gain confidence. And pay attention to the patterns of cards, because you will find that over time certain ones recur. Get to know them well.

ABOVE: *A card showing hexagram 13, (Tung Jen) from The I Ching of Love. Illustrated by artist Ma Nishavdo, it reproduces the 64 hexagrams of the ancient Chinese oracle. Its interpretations relate to love and relationships.*

Preparing For a Reading

In Tarot, ritual can help to calm the mind. Like laying the table before eating a meal, so you should prepare a clean surface and lay down the cloth in which you wrap your cards. Some Tarot readers light a candle before they begin, because this symbolizes passing from one state to the next; the candle is extinguished when the reading is over.

You can use the whole deck or just the major arcana cards. If the question you are asking is very important, use the major arcana because this will give you deeper interpretations, particularly if you are using fewer cards in your spread.

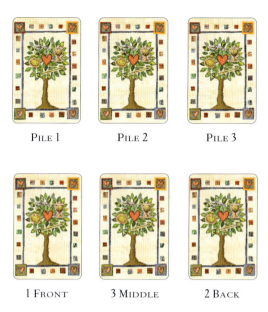

Cut the deck into three piles from left to right (see top row). Pile 2 goes to the back, pile 3 to the middle and pile 1 to the front.

Shuffle the cards as you think of a question or an event that you would like illuminated. If you do not have anything specific to ask, just allow your mind to wander. Take as long as you need, and stop shuffling when you feel calm and ready. Shuffling the deck is an important part of the Tarot ritual because it helps you focus your attention on the present—this is the yoga of Tarot practice. Then take the shuffled deck and, with your left hand (traditionally this represents the hand of fate), cut the deck into three piles. Replace the piles on top of one another, with the bottom one uppermost. If you are reading for someone else, ask them to shuffle and cut their own cards so that they imprint them with their personal energy.

Some readers shuffle and cut for their client. These are usually psychic readers, or "sensitives," who use the cards but do not actually need them because they can already "read" a client through their energy, or presence. To read intuitively for others, it is best to have the other person touch the cards before you lay them out. This is important because—particularly for meditative rather than purely predictive readings—Tarot is an interactive process. While you are learning to read the cards for friends, ask them what they think about your interpretation as you go. The idea of asking for a reading, and sitting before an oracle in fearful anticipation, is akin to visiting the doctor for a diagnosis without having any say in his or her recommendations for treatment. The relationship between the querent (the person undergoing the reading) and the reader is equal. The cards provide the stimulus for thought and illuminate choices.

Three-card Readings

Threes make a story: a beginning, middle, and end. You can start by using just three cards to create a Tarot story that describes the past, present, and future. Use this arrangement for an overview or to detail one aspect of life, such as career or relationships. Shuffle and cut the cards, then lay them out as shown.

1   2   3

Sample Reading: Relationships

Card 1: Past
Card 2: Present
Card 3: Future

1   2   3

The querent wanted to find out about future relationships as she had just left a long-term partner. The cards drawn are the Eight of Cups, the Nine of Cups, and the Knight of Swords.

The Eight of Cups is in the past position, which shows that there has been dissatisfaction in an established relationship, and that the querent was not getting what she needed from this partnership.

The Nine of Cups shows that she is now much happier and can have whatever she wishes for. This is a good time to meet a new partner.

Her future is the Knight of Swords in shining armor: a professional, charming individual who comes on the scene like a whirlwind. Events will speed up, and there is drama. To find out more about the Knight, we chose an additional card, the Ace of Wands. This can indicate great beginnings—travel and a family—so it is likely that the querent's new relationship will bring her excitement and passion.

Sample Reading: Travel

1

2

3

Card 1: Past
Card 2: Present
Card 3: Future

The querent has been thinking of taking time off from work and traveling around Asia. He wants to know how feasible his plans are. The cards drawn are the Eight of Wands, the Ace of Pentacles, and the Chariot.

The Eight of Wands is in the past position. This shows that he has made progress in his ambitions and has been presented with exciting opportunities, one of which concerns travel. He has lots of options available to him.

The Ace of Pentacles is in the present position. He has the money or, if not just at present, will find it very soon—a time of prosperity and success beckons.

The Chariot reveals that the querent will physically travel because his determination will make it possible. This important trip will bring him freedom and opportunity.

Sample Reading: Money, Work, and Love

Card 1: Money
Card 2: Career
Card 3: Love

1

2

3

The querent did not have a pressing question, so we used three cards for insight into her three key life areas: money, work, and love. The cards drawn are the Magician, the World, and the Emperor.

Because three major arcana cards have been drawn, important change can be expected. The Magician appears as the money card. While the querent is not well off, she has all the talent she needs to make money appear out of thin air. This is a creative time for her—her horizons are expanding.

The World is her career card. She is near the end of a particular phase of work; she may even be thinking of changing her career. She has been successful so far, but the start of a new enterprise is close at hand, and she can look forward to it.

The Emperor is the querent's love card. In a woman's reading, the Emperor often denotes her husband. Here, it represents her long-term partner, who could give her stability as she undergoes major changes in her career and finances.

The Heart and Head Spread

Card 4: The significator, or
heart of the matter
Card 1: Your spiritual self
Card 2: What you think
Card 3: What you feel

1

2

4

3

This simple spread uses the major arcana only. This reveals the spiritual, intellectual, and emotional aspects of your life, along with a central significator, or a card that acts as a key to the whole reading. It can be read predictively, but I find it a good spread for personal meditation too.

Remove all the minor arcana cards from the deck, then shuffle and cut the remaining twenty-two cards, laying them out as shown. Read the significator card first and interpret the other cards in the light of this.

Sample Reading: Leaving Work

The querent is taking early retirement from work and wants to look at a number of issues relating to the end of her present career. The cards drawn are the Chariot, Justice, the Hermit, and Temperance.

1

2

4

Card 4: The heart of the matter is Temperance. The querent is managing several situations that are potentially explosive. She is working hard, weighing up her finances until her layoff payment, and dealing with potentially precarious individuals whom she needs to rely on right now. She requires emotional balance during a stressful time.

38

CARD 1: The Chariot represents the querent's spirituality and her hopes for herself. This card reveals that she will make sure progress. It is likely she will travel in the future, by means of a vehicle, or generally spending more time away from home. New adventures await her, so she is looking forward to the next phase of her life.

CARD 2: Justice appears in the thinking position, which is apt given that the querent wants her decision to be justified, and wants to be fairly treated financially and have her past work acknowledged. She wants all legal agreements to be signed and sealed so that she can take up her chariot and move on.

CARD 3: The Hermit reveals how the querent feels. It shows that she feels a little alone on her path to seek the life that she wants. This can manifest as a desire for time out to recuperate after she leaves her job. The Hermit also reveals that things will take time. If we relate this card to Justice, then finalizing contracts may take a bit longer than expected.

SAMPLE READING: LOVE AND SECURITY

The querent has a good relationship with his partner, with whom he does not live. He would like some insight into issues of commitment for the future. The cards drawn are the Empress, the Sun, the Moon, and the Devil.

2

1

3

CARD 4: The heart of the matter is the Empress. This is the querent's partner. She represents home life and the desire for love, prosperity, and stability.

4

CARD 1: The Sun in this spiritual-self position reflects the querent's hopes for joy and security. The Sun card shows a sanctuary of happiness, the spiritual ideal of a relationship, and the protection it can bring. The querent wants a life in the sun in an environment in which he is looked after, perhaps by his partner.

CARDS 2 AND 3: The Devil appears in the thinking position, and the Moon reveals the querent's emotions. These two cards link with one another, because they reveal subconscious doubt and a practical awareness of a pending decision. The Moon shows an element of disillusion that his present relationship can be lived in the sun, which makes him fear restriction, as symbolized by the Devil. His partner may not be able to give him what he needs, and he must soon decide what is best for their relationship.

The Star Spread

Card 1: The present
Card 2: Feelings
Card 3: Thoughts
Card 4: Significator (the heart of the matter)
Card 5: The subconscious: what is hidden and will surface
Card 6: Your known desires
Card 7: The outcome

The Star is a popular spread with Tarot readers, and it can be particularly insightful when you use only the major arcana cards; this gives spreads such as this, which use fewer cards, a dedicated focus. Shuffle, cut, and lay out the cards as shown above. Interpret card 4, the significator or heart of the matter, before the other cards, as this anchors your reading.

Sample Reading: Will the Past Be Put to Rest?
The querent has been looking back at past issues that have been troubling her for some time. She wants to know if she can resolve and heal the past.

Card 4 (significator): The querent's significator card is the Tower. This reflects her present situation and emotions. It shows that her previous beliefs, and her perspective on a situation, are being demolished. She is experiencing a testing and even fearful time in her life; she may feel that she has little that is concrete to hold on to. However, this collapse of an ideal will liberate her thinking in the long term; it will just take a little more time.

CARD 1: This shows where the querent is at present, and here the Death card makes an appearance. She is dealing with an important ending in one aspect of her life; this may be her acknowledgment that she needs to let go of the past. There is also a natural inevitability about this card, so it is right that she should examine her present thoughts and feelings.

CARD 2: The card in this position represents the querent's feelings about her situation, here symbolized by the World. She feels that she is ready to move on, and that by rights she needs a fresh start.

CARD 3: The Hermit reflects how the querent has intellectualized her situation. The card shows that she has analyzed past issues in her own way, and has been on a personal quest to find an answer. This has taken up much of her time.

CARDS 5 AND 6: Card 5, the Devil, is the querent's subconscious at work. She will need to make a mature decision if she is to make progress; she may be tempted to stay where she is, perhaps repeating old patterns of behavior. This decision is important if she is to achieve the ambition of card 6, the Star, which reveals her known desires. She would love to feel inspired and hopeful, and revitalized rather than drained.

CARD 7: The Magician is a great card for this querent, because it shows that the outcome will be positive. The Magician is a wonderful symbol of energy, creativity, and in some cases travel; he deals with the present and looks to the future. Unlike the Hermit, the Magician shows off his talent to others, so it appears as if the querent finds a way to express herself as an individual rather than contemplate the past in the dark. She will move on and opportunities will beckon. Getting to this stage, however, feels like a long process just now, but if the querent has patience and self-belief, she can look forward to her future with optimism.

The Past, Present, and Future Spread

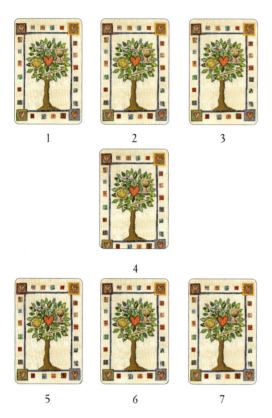

Card 1: The past
Card 2: How you saw yourself at this time
Card 3: What you learned
Card 4: Your present circumstances
Card 5: New influences about to enter your life
Card 6: How they will affect you
Card 7: The outcome

This seven-card spread is a good preliminary to the Celtic Cross (see page 45). The pattern of the spread consists of two three-card sequences for the past and future, with a single card for the present. Shuffle and cut the cards, dealing seven cards face down from the top of the deck as shown.

Variation

To get more information about a card you have already laid down, select four more cards from the top of the deck and lay them around your chosen card as shown overleaf. Read them in turn as described, as their meanings will provide four additional aspects of the situation.

Sample Reading: Career Overview

The querent did not have a specific question, but wanted a general overview of past, present, and future influences surrounding her career.

CARD 1: The past is represented by the Three of Wands. This shows that the querent's past work has been recognized by others. It is likely that she works in a creative field, or has had a good opportunity to express her ideas in her career.

CARDS 2 AND 3: The Hermit reveals how the querent saw herself at this time—what she felt and believed about her situation. She felt that she took an intellectual approach to her work, but this set her apart from others, since she looked within herself to find answers; she may have worked alone at home. What she learned is summarized by the Two of Pentacles, the need to find balance and solvency. This also indicates a good business partnership, which may have sparked new ideas, as represented by the next card, the Chariot.

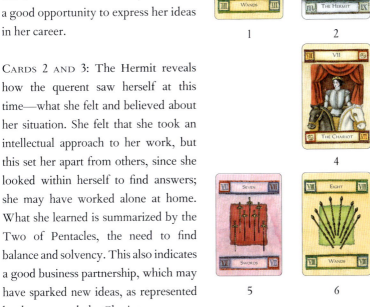

CARD 4: The querent's present circumstances are represented by the Chariot: through determined effort, she is forging ahead in her career. We laid four more cards around this one (see Variation, overleaf).

CARD 5: The Seven of Swords reveals new influences that are about to enter the querent's life. The Seven shows conflict and the need to use her intellect to negotiate some challenging situations.

CARD 6: The Eight of Wands illuminates the impact that these new events and feelings will have. It shows that the hard work of the Seven of Swords pays off, and she will be rewarded with lots of opportunities to shine, and possibly to travel.

CARD 7: The Seven of Pentacles is the outcome. The querent will need to stay focused and work hard for promotion. As the Three of Wands in the past has shown, there have been, and are, rewards along the way, but lots of effort will be needed at each stage. The message here is to persevere.

THE MYSTERY OF THE TAROT

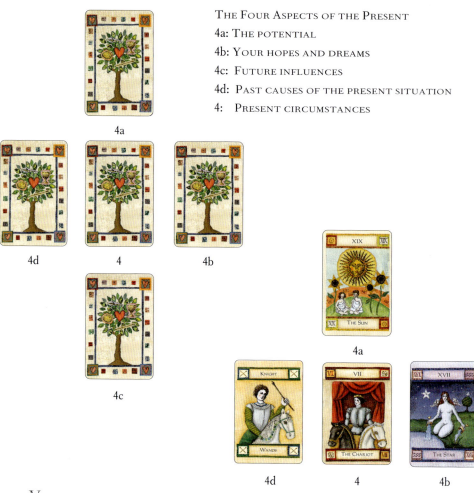

THE FOUR ASPECTS OF THE PRESENT
4a: THE POTENTIAL
4b: YOUR HOPES AND DREAMS
4c: FUTURE INFLUENCES
4d: PAST CAUSES OF THE PRESENT SITUATION
4: PRESENT CIRCUMSTANCES

VARIATION

Four additional cards were chosen to surround Card 4, the Chariot, because the querent wanted more insight into her present situation. The cards chosen were the Sun, the Star, the Knight of Cups, and the Knight of Wands. It is likely that the querent will see some rapid changes very soon, since the two Knights indicate the speeding up of events. She may have a job or new project that will further her ambitions. The Knight of Wands can also represent relocation, so she may move to a new job, or need to travel at short notice. This will provide satisfaction and inspiration, symbolized by the Sun and the Star. Under the Chariot is the Knight of Cups, an individual who may not be able to keep his promises. If this is a new boss, his dreamy nature may distract the querent from difficulties that await with the Seven of Swords, card 7 in the main reading.

44

THE TAROT READINGS

THE CELTIC CROSS

CARD 1: YOUR CURRENT CIRCUMSTANCES
CARD 2: WHAT IS HELPING OR HINDERING YOU
CARD 3: THE BEST YOU CAN EXPECT AT PRESENT
CARD 4: THE HIDDEN FACTORS AROUND YOU
CARD 5: THE EFFECT OF THE PAST
CARD 6: YOUR NEXT MOVE

CARD 7: HOW YOU SEE YOURSELF; WHAT YOU CAN DO
CARD 8: HOW OTHERS SEE YOU; HOW YOU RELATE TO THEM
CARD 9: HOPES AND FEARS
CARD 10: THE OUTCOME

The Celtic Cross is a traditional and popular spread that explores general life influences and events, and illuminates the different aspects of a specific question. This spread is named after its general shape and the pattern of cards 1 and 2, which express what complements or crosses you in life. Shuffle and cut the deck as usual, then deal ten cards from the top as shown. Interpret cards 1 and 2 first, because they reveal the motivation behind the reading; then cards 4 and 5, which give the background to the present situation; next interpret card 3; and then read cards 6–10, which look ahead.

Sample Reading: How Will My Work Be Received?

The querent is a painter who is nearing the end of a difficult commission. He wants to know if his work will be well received, and if more commissions will result. He needs to rest, but knows he must look for new work if he is going to survive financially.

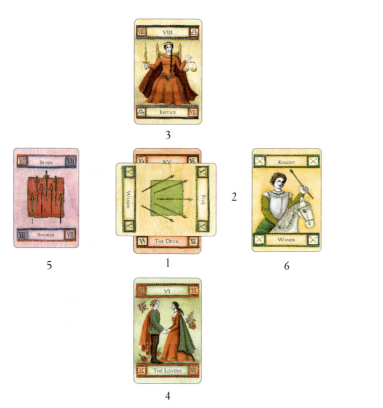

CARDS 1 AND 2: The Devil is crossed by the Five of Wands. The Devil shows that the querent feels tied to an unsatisfactory situation that is causing worry and conflict. The Five of Wands reveals that he is under pressure, and faces a situation that he has not previously encountered—which is why he does not know which way to turn. Together, these cards show that the querent has felt restricted and unrewarded in his work. The challenges of this commission are new to him—he may be dealing with a difficult and demanding client. There may also be a problem with a contract here; if so, it is important that he takes action now, and begins by re-checking every detail of any important paperwork.

46

CARDS 4 AND 5: The Lovers and the Seven of Swords looks at past circumstances and any hidden elements that may be contributing to the present situation. The Lovers shows that the querent has made a commitment to himself and his work, and may have taken a risk to do so. The Swords card indicates a past confrontation or harrowing negotiation prior to the work beginning, which has now magnified in the form of the central card, the Devil.

CARD 3: Justice is the best that the querent can hope for at this time—he will be fairly treated in a testing situation, and any contractual issues should be finalized to his satisfaction. He will feel that any action taken by him regarding his client will be justified: it is therefore likely that his work will be accepted, but he will make a resolution not to dwell on past difficulties of the work, and look ahead.

CARD 6: The querent's next move is represented by the Knight of Wands. This reveals that events will speed up, and new offers of work should arrive. The Wands are cards of creativity, so this indicates that he has no need to worry about being out of employment for too long.

CARD 7: The Star reveals how the querent will see himself at this time. He will find his muse again as he puts the present situation behind him. He can recover his creativity and inspiration.

CARD 8: The card in position 8 shows attitudes around the querent, and the general influences impacting upon him. He will feel at one with the world, and feel happier and more secure financially, symbolized by the Sun. He may also take a well-earned vacation to sunnier climes. Other people will respond positively to him, perhaps offering him the sanctuary of their home for a short holiday.

CARD 9: The Four of Wands reveals the querent's hopes and fears. This card shows that he can hope for appreciation and establishment.

CARD 10: The outcome to the querent's present situation is represented by the Four of Swords. This shows a time for healing and recuperation after struggle—so the querent will be able to rest after an intense period of work. In this sense, the Four of Swords is a continuation of the idea of card 8, the Sun: a tranquil haven.

We can also look at the combined meaning of the two Fours here, cards 9 and 10. Two fours together traditionally indicate that there will be a good time of stability ahead.

The Tree of Life Spread

Card 1: Kether: spiritual influences
Card 2: Chokmah: what is to be realized
Card 3: Binah: what will nurture you
Card 4: Chesed: planning and the law
Card 5: Geburah: hopes
Card 6: Tipereth: harmony
Card 7: Netzach: romance and desire
Card 8: Hod: thoughts
Card 9: Yesod: instinct
Card 10: Malkuth: what grounds you
Variation: optional significator card (s): wellbeing and balance

1

2

3

4

5

(S), optional

6

7

8

9

10

This meditative spread is helpful when you have a lot going on in your life. Like the Celtic Cross, it assists you in separating life themes and events into specific areas. This simplified spread is based on the Tree of Life, the core symbol of kabbala (see page 24). Each card represents a sephirot, or energy center, on the Tree, which has various interpretations, just some of which are given here. The meaning of the card positions is more detailed than for many Tarot spreads, so you need to combine your understanding of each sephirot with the individual card meanings. Shuffle and split the deck as previously described (see page 35), then lay out ten cards in the sequence shown.

Variation

You can also add a significator card to the spread. Deal this card last and place it directly under card 1, kether. This represents the sephirot daath. Daath relates to your wellbeing and spiritual development—this is how you balance heaven and earth.

Sample Reading: Relocation

The querent has two homes. She is hoping to sell her city apartment to move to a larger home in the countryside, which she has already bought. She wanted some clarity on the million and one demands on her time as a single person dealing with relocation. For this reading, the querent chose not to select a significator card.

1

3

2

5

4

6

8

7

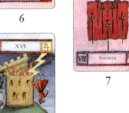

9

Card 1: Spiritual influences around you

The Seven of Cups shows that the querent has a bewildering number of decisions to make, but must choose one path. Her imagination is consequently in overdrive.

Card 2: What is to be realized

This card position also shows the querent's relationship with the men in her life. The Six of Cups reveals reunions with old friends and those people from her past who, in helping with her new home, are helping her create her future. The querent is taking the good things from her past experiences and making them work for her—literally.

10

Card 3: What will nurture you

This card position also shows the querent's relationship with women in her life. The Three of Cups reveals that she will soon be celebrating some good news and meeting supportive female friends in her new location.

Card 4: Planning and the law

Temperance shows that the querent needs to look after the detail just now—she must tend the balance of her life, managing two homes in two locations until her city apartment is sold. She will soon be dealing with contracts and other legal affairs. She will manage this, but she is also mindful of her new responsibilities.

Card 5: Hopes

The Seven of Wands shows that the querent hopes that all her hard work will pay off. She may meet some competition along the way or experience a minor delay to her plans, so her work ethic is realistic in the circumstances.

Card 6: Harmony

The position of card 6 also reveals what is in the querent's heart. Here, she has the Ace of Swords reversed, showing a time of frustration and delay before she can relax and enjoy her new home. However, the card in this position may simply outline her fears about being held up, because the surrounding cards are very positive.

Card 7: Romance and desire

The Eight of Swords shows restriction on the romantic front, which is not surprising given that all the querent's energy is being dedicated to work and home at this time. The message here is to loosen up; she will meet a partner should she genuinely choose to.

Card 8: Thoughts

The Three of Pentacles shows tradespeople. The meaning of this card is the building of a little empire, which applies to both home and business. The querent will soon be dealing with builders through whom her ideas can take shape.

Card 9: Instinct

The Tower is the querent's instinct card. On a practical level, she is leaving a safe fortress for the unknown and she feels vulnerable. Emotionally she is fragile too, because her natural defences are down as she deals with the fallout of leaving a part of her life behind. The collapse of the tower, however, is blameless and unavoidable, so the insecurity she may be feeling now is perhaps the aftershock that follows a life-changing decision. It can also represent a fear that everything will fall apart.

Card 10: What grounds you

This position can be reinterpreted as a question: what makes you feel grounded? The Page of Cups signals the answer: invitations, conversations, and ideas. The Tower collapses, but the world still turns. The querent will receive good news and hear about opportunities that will build up her confidence.

The Horseshoe Spread

CARD 1: The past
CARD 2: The present
CARD 3: Future conditions
CARD 4: The best path to follow
CARD 5: Attitudes around you
CARD 6: Obstacles
CARD 7: The outcome

This is a classic spread to call on when you need an answer to a specific question. The Horseshoe can have either five or seven cards; a seven-card reading is shown here. Shuffle and cut the cards as usual, then lay them out as shown.

Sample Reading: Will My Finances Improve?

The querent has had to take out loans to finance his debts. He is self-employed and needs to pay tax in the coming months, and is doubtful if he can keep up his repayments. The cards chosen are the Ace of Pentacles, the Seven of Wands, the Ace of Swords, the Three of Pentacles, the Empress, the Ten of Wands, and the Moon.

CARD 1: The Ace of Pentacles shows that the querent has been successful with money in the past. He may have had a windfall or other cash gift.

CARD 2: The present shows the Seven of Wands: he is fighting off demands on his time and money, and will need to work hard to get the security that he hopes for.

CARD 3: The Ace of Swords reveals that the querent will succeed; the prevailing circumstances are good.

CARD 4: The Three of Pentacles shows that craftsmanship will help him. This means attention to detail, hard work, and creativity. Putting words into action will be important.

CARD 5: The Empress reveals that others will be generous and understanding. The downside of this card is that people may assume that the querent is not struggling, since they are used to him being financially capable.

CARD 6: The Ten of Wands predicts that the querent may be overburdened with responsibility. This may also reflect his attitude: things may get on top of him and he may feel paralyzed by indecision, rather than driven to act to resolve his debts.

CARD 7: The outcome is the Moon, which reveals a crisis of faith and indecision, as indicated by the previous card. The querent therefore needs to act now to improve his situation, rather than wait until the repayments become a serious burden. The Ace of Swords shows that he can extricate himself from his debt and win, but steering clear of panic will be by far his best defence.

1

7

6

2

3

5

4

THE TAROT READINGS

Timing Spreads:
The Year Ahead Spread

CARDS 1–12: CARD 1 REPRESENTS THE FIRST
MONTH FROM THE DATE OF THE READING

CARD 2: THIS SHOWS THE EVENTS OF THE
NEXT MONTH, AND SO ON FOR TWELVE
MONTHS

CARD 13: THE SIGNIFICATOR, WHICH
REVEALS THE TONE OF THE YEAR AHEAD

THE MYSTERY OF THE TAROT

In the Year Ahead Spread, one card is laid out for each month of the year, plus a central significator, card 13. After shuffling and cutting the deck as usual, the first card from the top of the deck is placed in the nine o'clock position, followed by the others in a counterclockwise direction as shown.

SAMPLE READING: WHAT THE NEXT YEAR HOLDS

The querent wanted a sense of what the next twelve months had in store, in terms of her work and social life.

54

CARD 13 (SIGNIFICATOR): The significator is the Five of Wands. This shows the need for the querent to stand firm and stay true to her principles, regardless of external pressures. It reveals an eventful but testing twelve months ahead.

CARD 1: Month one has the Seven of Pentacles, which represents ongoing work and the potential for success. In her career and new home, the querent needs to persevere.

CARD 2: In month two, the Page of Wands brings some welcome fun and fresh inspiration. The querent will soon hear about an opportunity, but she needs to be practical too, and resist the temptation to take on too much too soon.

CARDS 3, 4, 5, AND 6: The next four months reveal a run of major arcana cards initiated by Death, which shows an ending and a new beginning. The querent will undergo some major changes during this time as she leaves behind one way of living. Justice shows that she is rewarded morally and will be dealt with fairly; legal issues will be resolved to her liking. The Hermit heralds a time to recuperate, and an element of delay. She will be eager to move forward but is held back, although this provides an opportunity to process recent events and learn from her experiences. The Strength card shows that she will need to be patient, and even emotionally strong in order to support others.

CARD 7: Month seven sees the end of a testing time. Inspiration, energy, and success arrive as the querent begins to feel at one with the rest of the world. The Star brings creative opportunities and vitality. Her dream will come true.

CARD 8: Month eight brings the Two of Cups and an intimate partnership, born from the happy environment of the previous card, the Star. If this is not a romantic alliance, then the querent will meet a new friend who becomes a soulmate.

CARD 9: Month nine is a time to look forward to, as friendship, celebrations, and light-heartedness prevail with the Three of Cups.

CARD 10: Month ten reveals the Four of Pentacles, showing proud achievement, satisfaction, and deserved rewards for work.

CARD 11: Month eleven brings the Ace of Pentacles; this will be a great time for career and money, so a pay rise may be given or an unexpected check arrive.

CARD 12: Month twelve shows a reversal of the good fortune of the Ace, but this may be perception, not reality. She may fear that she will be left out somehow, after her months of hard work. This will not be the case; there will be a chance to put right any wrong.

The Month Ahead Spread

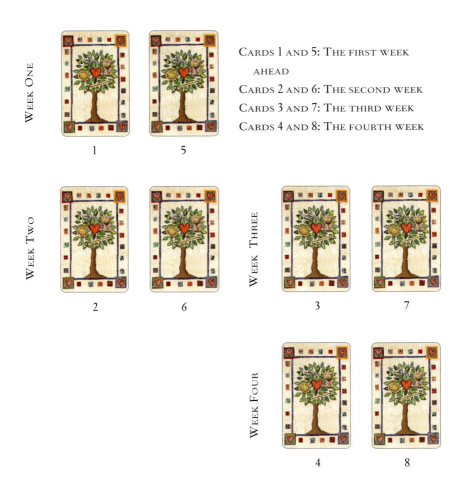

Cards 1 and 5: The first week ahead
Cards 2 and 6: The second week
Cards 3 and 7: The third week
Cards 4 and 8: The fourth week

Laying two cards for each week gives you two aspects for a broader interpretation. Shuffle and cut the deck as usual, following the layout shown.

Sample Reading: Work For the Next Four Weeks

The querent wanted to know how her work would progress over the next month. She had submitted some ideas to her manager, and was hoping that she would soon have some positive feedback.

Week one: The cards drawn are the Six of Cups and the Ace of Pentacles. This will be a profitable and possibly innovative week workwise, symbolized by the Ace; the querent will be feeling balanced and settled, signified by the Six.

WEEK TWO: The Nine of Cups and the Star show that it is likely that she will be recognized for her ideas. The Nine is also the "wish" card, so whatever she wishes for now can become a reality.

WEEK THREE: The Eight of Swords and Temperance reveal that now the querent needs to put her ideas into action, although this creates a sense of restriction. There may be some testing negotiations ahead; an offer from her manager or a client won't give her much room for maneuver. All she can do here is temper her emotions, and aim to manage difficult people and situations with skill and consideration.

WEEK FOUR: The Four of Cups shows that the querent will feel that her life is back in kilter, but there may also be a trace of irritation or boredom—maybe because issues from week two do not get resolved. This may escalate into a battle, shown by the Three of Swords. Suffering painful disappointment may be the only way to get to the heart of a problem and subsequently resolve it.

The Week Ahead Spread

This spread is an ideal way to gain insight into an important week ahead. Shuffle and cut the cards as usual, then lay them out following the arrangement shown, beginning with the significator card. Interpret this card first to get a feel for the whole seven days, then interpret each of the other cards in turn.

Sample Reading: What the Next Week Has in Store

The querent wanted to see how she would prosper financially, creatively, and socially during the week ahead.

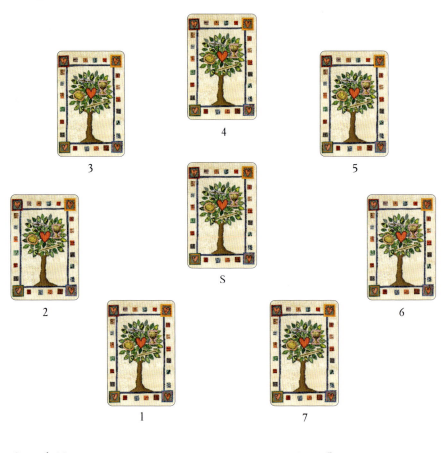

Card 1: Monday
Card 2: Wednesday
Card 3: Friday
Card 4: Sunday

Card 5: Tuesday
Card 6: Thursday
Card 7: Saturday
S: Significator card

THE SIGNIFICATOR (S): The significator card is the Ten of Wands. This foretells an incredibly busy week; the querent may take on too much and feel overburdened with responsibility (some readers prefer to shuffle and cut the cards again when this card arrives: see page 140). However, the overall outlook—given the spread of cards—is very positive.

MONDAY (1): The Eight of Wands brings great news and happiness. This is an auspicious day for work and expressing her talents.

TUESDAY (5): The Knight of Pentacles reveals that Tuesday is fortuitous for getting things done. It may not be inspiring, but progress is assured.

WEDNESDAY (2): Judgment symbolizes the summing up of a series of events before moving on. It is likely that the querent is coming to the end of a project, and will mentally assess what has been achieved.

3: FRIDAY

4: SUNDAY

5: TUESDAY

2: WEDNESDAY

S: SIGNIFICATOR

6: THURSDAY

1: MONDAY

7: SATURDAY

59

THURSDAY (6): The Ten of Cups shows great reward and joy, which is usually connected with a community or group of people such as family, friends, or work colleagues. It brings success and achievement, so this is a great day for social gatherings and celebrations.

FRIDAY (3): The Chariot. After the summing up of Wednesday and Thursday's happy endings, Friday sees the querent take up the reins once more to move forward. This should be a day of energy and determined action; the card can also indicate a literal journey, so the querent may take a short trip.

SATURDAY (7): The Three of Cups crowns the sixth day, bringing harmony and love. It shows babies and children; in work terms, this is renewal and the seeds of a new venture. There will be socializing, too.

SUNDAY: (4) The Nine of Cups is the card drawn for Sunday. This Nine is traditionally the "wish" card of the minor arcana (see page 138), so this is a day on which the querent's dreams can come true. She will have the energy to enjoy socializing, so this should be a wonderful day on which she can feel genuinely positive about life; she can relax and appreciate all that she has achieved.

What to Do if You Cannot Make Sense of a Reading

If the cards that are first laid out for a reading just don't feel right, and you cannot get into an interpretative flow, bear in mind the following:

1. You can ask the querent to shuffle and cut the deck again. What inevitably happens is that salient cards from the first reading reappear in the second reading. This may sound unconvincing, but try this for yourself when you are self-reading and cannot attune to the cards you draw. A sign that reshuffling needs to be done is when the Ten of Wands arises; this often means that there is just too much going on, and the querent needs more time to consider his or her question by reshuffling the cards.

2. Just because you cannot intuit the relationships between cards in a spread does not always mean that the person for whom you are reading cannot; only they know what is really going on in their lives. Write down your reading for them, and at a later date ask if anything that you interpreted came about. This process will give you the confidence to keep going with a reading when you feel unsure, or to know that next time you could ask the querent to reshuffle the cards.

3. You may feel hesitant if the cards are "bad": the Tower, the Devil, or Death, for example. Although they might seem traumatic, these cards often signal release and new beginnings. Within each is the gift of action and necessary change. And consider that, for some querents, the opportunity to talk about difficult situations is a release in itself.

4. Interpreting the Cards
The Major Arcana

The twenty-two cards of the major arcana are numbered from 0 to XXI. The sequence can be seen as a quest for self-knowledge; alongside the individual meanings of the cards, the major arcana cards that we draw in a reading are indicative of a stage in our thinking and spiritual development. The Tarot journey begins with card 0, the Fool, and starts again with card XXI, the World; it is a continuous cycle of birth and regeneration. The innocent Fool experiences the other twenty-one cards as landmarks and tests as he seeks completion—the integration of mind, body, and spirit that is symbolized by the World.

The Fool's Story
Discovery: The Fool to the Chariot

The Fool is zero, an innocent who sets the wheel of the Tarot cycle in motion. He encounters I, the Magician, the alchemist who shows him the magical potential at his fingertips. With the Fool's growing awareness of his environment, he then turns his attention to his earthly and spiritual parents. These are II, the High Priestess—the goddess aspect of his mother—and III, the Empress, who takes care of his earthly needs. Similarly,

his father the Emperor, IV, makes the rules; the Emperor's spiritual counterpart, the Hierophant, V, gives him an education. Card VI, the Lovers, is the first test of the Fool's autonomy, for he must choose between the parental bond and a relationship with a partner. When he meets the Chariot, VII, he realizes his freedom and risks dealing with the world alone.

The Moral Lessons: Justice to Temperance

The Fool now encounters four moral lessons; Justice, the Hermit, Strength, and Temperance. In Justice, VIII, he meets Fortuna, goddess of destiny; he is judged by

others. The Hermit, IX, teaches him how to be alone and seek out what he needs, away from his peers. In Strength, XI, the Fool learns gentleness when dealing with external opponents and internal conflict. Temperance, XIV, heralds the spiritual alchemist, and so the Fool learns to control his temperament and quantify the elements of his life; he must balance the needs of his family. Woven within these four lessons, the Fool must also experience Death, XIII, which brings both endings and beginnings; his subconscious fears and the flow of life in the Wheel of Fortune, X; and he must be prepared to make a sacrifice, which is symbolized by card XII, the Hanged Man.

From Darkness to Light: The Devil to the World

The Fool's darkness is a power struggle between his lower instincts and his higher nature. He meets card XV, the Devil, and so greets temptation: having to choose between greed and generosity, lust and love. His success depends on his maturity. Yet whatever he envisages as being within his control, life has other plans. The Tower of his ego, XVI, collapses to make way for his connection to heavenly inspiration, in the form of the Star, XVII. Here, he realizes his personal goals, which are nourished in the creative sanctuary of the Sun, XIX. Yet his journey is not yet complete. As the Fool has

moved from the twilight of the Star to the full heat of the Sun, so he has had to endure the disillusion of the light of the Moon, XVIII, which exposes his deepest fears. He must again make a difficult decision that will ensure his progress. Judgment, XX, is the Fool's final calling to judge himself. He knows that his journey is almost complete. He has the World, XXI, to discover, all over again.

A

Meditation on the Figure-of-eight

The figure-of-eight, or lemniscate, appears prominently on two major arcana cards: the Magician and Strength. It is also evident in the Hermit's hourglass and on the Two of Pentacles in some decks; and, in the Rider Waite deck, on the crossed arms of the man

THE MYSTERY OF THE TAROT

ABOVE: *The World, probably dating from fifteenth-century Italy, bears a similarity to the World card of the Visconti-Sforza deck (see page 108).*

on the Nine of Cups. In the Marseilles deck, the crossed legs of the Emperor and the hermaphrodite figure on the World card imply the figure-of-eight formation.

The figure-of-eight is an ancient infinity symbol. It is also a kind of Tarot DNA, because it represents the flow of energy created by the tension between two opposite poles.

Tarotist Alfred Douglas uses the figure-of-eight as a way to examine the relationships between the cards of the major arcana. The cards are laid out in a figure-of-eight shape (see opposite, page 65). The upper loop of cards points outward and the lower loop inward, with the Wheel of Fortune and the World crossing in the center. These cards represent the midpoint and end of the Tarot journey. The upper loop symbolizes the self and our relationship with the outside world; the cards of the lower loop reveal introversion and our relationship with ourselves.

Each card in the upper loop has a counterpart in the lower loop, which can give the upper-loop card greater context. If you discover a pair of cards in a spread that relate in this way, it can aid your interpretation. For example, the beginning of the inner journey is signaled by the Hermit. His counterpart is Strength, who introduces the feminine qualities of gentleness to balance the Hermit's analytical masculinity. Strength is also what the Hermit will need while he is alone in the wilderness.

REVERSED AND UPRIGHT MEANINGS

Generally, when a card appears in a reversed position (turned upside down) its meanings are more negative than when it appears in an upright position. However, in the case of cards whose upright meanings are negative (such as the Tower and the Five of Pentacles), the opposite is true: the reversed meanings are more positive because the querent is usually further along the path to recovery.

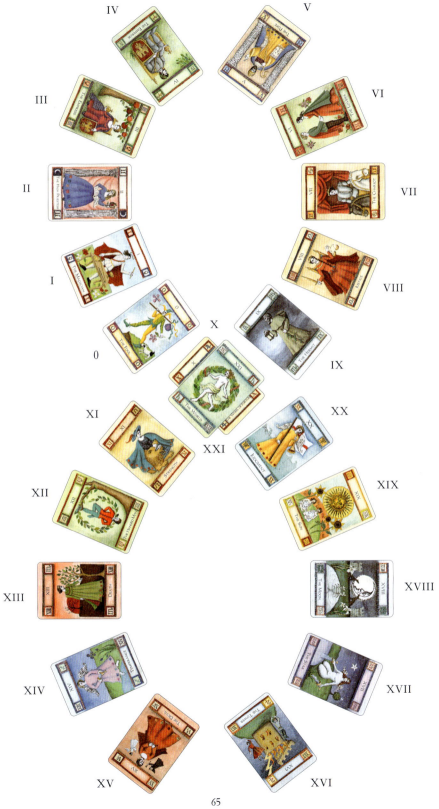

0 The Fool

The Jester

The Fool is innocence. Poised to leap between one world and another, he risks the spiritual unknown from Earth to thin air. In modern playing cards, the Fool survives as the joker, or jester. As the court jester can often articulate subtle or difficult truths, so the Tarot Fool may make his entrance into a reading to remind you of the intemperance and absurdity of life. And, as the jester plays off the crowd, so it has been suggested that he is set to experience the collective journey of all the cards in the major arcana cycle.

Symbolism

The Visconti-Sforza Fool is depicted as a beggar wearing thin robes; he has seven chicken feathers in his hair. These symbolize the poverty of his experience as he begins his journey. Tarot historians also assign the Fool as a symbol of Lent because he has surrendered his worldly goods. Modern decks depict the Fool wearing three jester's bells on his hat and two on his boots, totaling five. Five is the number of mankind, which here signifies folly of a human kind. The dog (see page 30) worries at the Fool's heels, a warning of danger ahead. The Fool carries a small bag for a great journey; it contains little but his hopes for adventure. In some decks the Fool carries a flower or is entranced by a butterfly, which act as symbols of his naive hopes and of his need to discover the wider world for himself.

Astrology

The unnumbered Fool is an anomaly, a zero because his potential is yet to be realized. His element is Air. As the Fool steps off the Earth and into the ether to fulfill his quest, he gives himself up to wherever the wind will take him. His planet is Uranus, symbolizing independence.

Upright Meaning: Beginnings

A fresh start; freedom from the constraints of the past; release from a pattern of events and risk—provided you can enjoy the freefall rather than expect a soft landing. With this vital opportunity comes caution, exemplified by the Fool's faithful dog, so temper your idealism with practicality. As the jester, he can herald a beguiling character who brings innocence and fun.

Reversed Meaning: Irresponsibility

In the reversed position, the negative traits of the Fool come to the fore. Naivety turns to immaturity and irresponsibility, warning that a spontaneous decision needs a rethink. A business venture, plans for a new property or a whirlwind relationship may dissolve due to lack of foresight. He may also represent the literal Fool. This free spirit turns your world upside down and then, like a true idiot, reneges on his promises.

Card Combinations

The upright interpretation of the Fool may be modified if he appears as one of the last cards that you lay out in a spread. In this instance he would show the completion of the journey. To reveal whether his appearance is fortuitous or foolish, look at the nature of the surrounding cards in a reading:

The Fool with the Star	The Fool with the Moon
An inspired risk; a creative or spiritual quest	Impulsiveness leads to a confidence crisis; action before due thought

I The Magician

The Magus

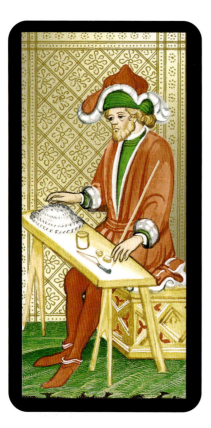

The Magician is a creative conjuror, active in his magic. The High Priestess keeps her knowledge to herself, but the Magician performs in public. In early Tarot decks such as the Visconti-Sforza, he may be seen seated at work, whereas later decks such as the Rider Waite show him standing by his table, with one hand pointing toward the Earth while the other holds aloft the baton or magic wand. These are the two faces of the Magician: the channeler of energy from the Earth to be woven to his will, and the everyday artisan. When reversed, he descends to the traveling charlatan who, through sleight of hand, deceives and mystifies.

Symbolism

The Magician makes magic from the energies of the four elements or minor arcana. On his table are the four suit symbols: pentacle, cup, sword, and wand; all are at his disposal. In the Visconti-Sforza and Marseilles decks, he is depicted as an artisan and the four suits are shown as everyday implements. He holds a baton, and on his table are a plain cup, a knife, and some coins. In Italy, the Magician was originally known as *Il Bagatto*, "cobbler" in the Milanese dialect. In the Soprafino Tarot (Milan, 1835) and the Dotti Tarot (Milan, 1845), for example, the implements on his table are those of the cobbler at work.

The lemniscate, or figure-of-eight for infinity (see page 63) shown above his head or in the form of a lazy eight in his hat denotes his understanding and knowledge. Around his waist is

a belt, sometimes referred to as a serpent-girdle. The serpent holds its tail in its mouth, which is also a symbol of alchemy, revealing renewal. The Magician's wand is yellow, representing intellect, and the card number is 1, for primal energy.

Astrology

The Magician's planet is Mercury, ruler of communication. Also known as Hermes, the winged messenger of Greek myth, Mercury was the Roman god of magic. In its form of quick-silver, mercury is also associated with transformation, the essence of magic.

Upright Meaning: Human Magic

You have everything you need at your fingertips to create now whatever you choose. This is a card of words and action rather than contemplation, a call to confidence and self-expression. The Magician's charmed influence indicates travel and creative projects, communication and integrity. This is therefore an auspicious card for anyone involved in business dealings. You can have it all; you just need to see what lies before you. Start with one telephone call or email, and everything else will fall into place as if by magic.

Reversed Meaning: Trickery

The Magician reversed warns of cheating and false appearances, dreams without foundation, and even self-delusion. A situation or individual is not what you think. For artists, he can manifest as a creative block. This may feel like a downturn in energy. If you feel at the bottom of a spiral, treat this as a mishap, not a life drama. Rather than spend more precious energy trying to fix the flaws, take time away from the situation.

Card Combinations

It is helpful to take note of the minor arcana cards that appear with the Magician in a reading. Because he has the four suit emblems before him, the suit or suits that surround him can reveal the way in which his influence will be expressed:

The Magician with the Ace of Pentacles	The Magician with the Queen of Cups
New financial opportunities; prosperity	New relationships; happiness

THE MYSTERY OF THE TAROT

II THE HIGH PRIESTESS

THE PAPESS

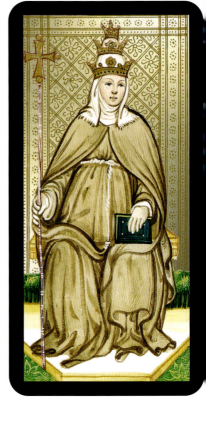

The High Priestess is the archetype of passive femininity, the keeper of wisdom that is not easily expressed. She is not of words, but of experience, intuition, and dreams. She represents learning and mediation between opposites. In a reading, her appearance signals both overt and covert feelings, and guides you toward listening to your inner voice in order to move forward. She is the natural counterpart of card V, the Hierophant, but her earthly expression can be seen in the next card in the sequence, the Empress, or mother earth.

SYMBOLISM

The High Priestess holds a book and sometimes a pomegranate or flower, which are lush symbols of her developed learning. The book, or scroll depicted in some decks, represents the Torah, Judaism's sacred book of hidden wisdom. The veil behind her shows that she is in touch with unconscious and conscious feelings. The two pillars are from the Tree of Life. On the Rider Waite deck, they bear a B on the left-

hand pillar and a J on the right. These initials stand for Boaz, representing the elements of Water and Earth, and Jachin, for Fire and Air. Boaz and Jachin are names on the pillars in Solomon's Temple that relate to kabbalistic tarot (see page 24). The two pillars also reflect her number, II, revealing the balance and opposition of co-dependent elements.

ASTROLOGY

The Moon is the planet of the High Priestess, signifying the inner world of secrets, emotion, and hidden wisdom. The waxing and waning moons link her with feminine, cyclic nature. The crescent moon represents expansion, the waning moon decline.

70

Upright Meaning: Intuition

Be guided by intuition. Take note of your dreams; nurture your desire for learning and seek out inspiration. In this aspect, the High Priestess is the teaching of your instinct. The duality of her number, II, may also indicate the need to choose between two courses of action. Take time to make this decision; listen to those who have the appropriate wisdom and experience. Their words are genuine, and may help you heal a private conflict before it becomes a moral dilemma.

Reversed Meaning: Secrets Revealed

In this position, the High Priestess shows that a secret is about to be revealed. With this, emotions surface and you may discover that your faith has been misplaced. A trusted authority figure, such as a spiritual advisor, educator, or manager, fails you by giving you wrong information or a wrong impression. Make no decision under pressure—give yourself more time.

Card Combinations

With the Moon, a confidence crisis concerning a woman is revealed, or the need for intuitive guidance to make a key decision. With the Hanged Man, a spiritual perspective changes your viewpoint and calls for time away from a situation.

The Female Pope

In the Visconti-Sforza deck, the High Priestess was thought to have been painted in the likeness of Maria Visconti, a relative of the Visconti family of northern Italy (see page 9) who commissioned the cards to commemorate the marriage of Bianca Maria Visconti and Francesco Sforza in 1441. Maria Visconti was a member of a Gnostic sect, the Guglielmites, and, according to some sources, was known as Sister Manfreda (Maifreda da Pirovano), a nun of the Order of the Humiliati. The High Priestess wears the habit of the Order, who were famous in western Europe for their wool cloth.

The Guglielmites were founded by a woman, Guglielma of Bohemia (d. 1281), and inspired by the prophecies of a twelfth-century Calabrian abbot, Joachim da Fiore. The sect believed that Christ would return in the year 1300, heralding a new age in which women could take the mantle of Pope. In readiness, Maria Visconti was chosen as the first female Pope, when she would officiate a mass at Santa Maria Maggiore, Rome. However, before she could fulfill her unorthodox calling she was burned at the stake for heresy in the fall of 1300.

III The Empress

The Empress is an earth mother. Serene and full-figured, she represents potential being fulfilled: close and happy relationships, nurturing, and sensitivity. She is a goddess of love but in very human form, and all benefit from her magnanimity. She expresses herself through dialogue and her relationships with others. Whereas the High Priestess is the private, intuitive aspect of femininity, the Empress is the brighter aspect whose creativity is evident through her children and consort, the Emperor, and her connection to nature as a whole.

Symbolism

In the Visconti-Sforza deck the Empress is crowned, which in later esoteric decks such as the Rider Waite and Sacred Rose is transformed into a diadem of twelve stars. This represents the twelve signs of the zodiac and months of the year. The eagle, the masculine protection symbol on her shield, is the emblem of the Roman Empire that appears on the Emperor card. Birds are also symbols of the soul so the eagle reveals the Empress as the essence, or soul, of the Earth. The apple denotes female sexuality, linking her to biblical Eve, who chose knowledge of life over perfection. The apple tree symbolizes an abundance of giving and receiving. In the Visconti-Sforza deck, the Empress's hands are green (see page 31) — the green fingers that make the garden grow. Her number is dynamic III, representing the triad of creation: mother, father, child.

Astrology

The Empress is associated with Venus, planet of love and fertility. Venus is concerned with what you value — relationships, material comfort, sensuousness, and sensitivity.

The Grain Mother and the Dog Star

The Tarot's Empress is the Great Mother, or mother-goddess, worshiped by every culture as a symbol of divine creativity and earthly fertility. Representing renewal and nature, she is depicted on the Rider Waite deck with corn, for the abundance of harvest. The Empress's planet, Venus, is also the Roman goddess of sexuality and love, revered as Aphrodite in ancient Greece and as Demeter, meaning "mother earth" or "grain mother." In Egypt the mother-goddess was Isis, linked with Sirius, the star whose rise brought the Inundation of the Nile and with it the survival of crops. The Great Mother as Isis is evocative of card II, the High Priestess; some decks depict her with a headdress of cow's horns and the Moon, the traditional attributes of Isis found on early figurines. Like the High Priestess, Isis is classically envisioned in blue robes, denoting spiritual attainment. In this context, she is a synthesis of the High Priestess and the Empress, as she is both earthly mother to her child, Horus, and goddess of the Egyptian pantheon.

Upright Meaning: Abundance

Giving and receiving love comes naturally; money goes and comes around, bringing prosperity and material comfort. You are supported and cherished as a child, and can give to others unconditionally. The Empress can also predict a new relationship or a pregnancy, and the positive influence of a mother-figure. This is a card of reassurance; know that you will grow and not falter in whatever you choose to do.

Reversed Meaning: Insecurity

Mothering becomes smothering when the Empress turns. Domestic bliss turns to chaos, so this card reveals unhappiness at home. The thrust of the reversed Empress is scarcity rather than abundance, so you may feel that you can never have enough of what you need to sustain you — affection, money, and support. The root of this may be a mother-figure whose insecurity leads her to resort to clinginess or emotional blackmail. Reassurance will soothe the discord, but equally it may be important to distance yourself during this influence. She can also point to infertility, and in general to a lack of positive emotion.

Card Combinations

With the Ace of Cups, a relationship or pregnancy that brings happiness is revealed. With Temperance, the needs of a family may be a source of tension.

IV The Emperor

The Emperor sits on the throne of authority. His qualities are traditionally masculine: martialism (in some decks he wears a suit of silver armor), rationalism, and virility. He can be depicted in a desert; the lack of water, which symbolizes the emotions, establishes that reason, not feeling, rules him. His natural consort, the Empress, represents love, whereas the Emperor reveals power. In this sense, he can be perceived as uninspiring or oppressive, a law-maker. Yet the Emperor also deals in the immediate present, taking what is before him at face value. In this sense, his heralds a time when we must take ourselves out into the wider, practical world.

Symbolism

The Emperor sits upright, in ready defence of the realm, sometimes holding an orb and scepter or wand. His shield shows earthly stability, and is emblazoned with the insignia of the black eagle, which denotes protection and masculine energy. His throne, also known as the cubit stone, symbolizes ultimate stability. In the Visconti-Sforza deck, the Emperor wears the ducal family crown, which is shown with decorative foliage. His number, IV, is the number of structure and civilization. On early cards such as the Cary-Yale Visconti-Sforza, the Emperor is surrounded by four pages, who bear allegiance to his rulership. His white beard represents wisdom.

Astrology

The Emperor's sign is Aries, the Ram. Aries is ruled by Mars, a reminder of the Emperor's martial qualities as a defender of his kingdom.

Upright Meaning: Fatherhood, Protection

The help of a father-figure, paternal love, and protection. This man will act, not pontificate, so his influence in a reading can reveal a life partner, guardian or parent, or someone in your life with decisive drive and ambition. He is also a natural rule-maker; as a parent, he sets the boundaries, so his appearance in a reading can show a requirement to conform. For women, the Emperor can foretell a partner to whom tradition and authority are important. This can be comforting or suffocating, depending on your standpoint.

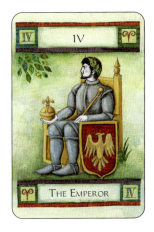

Reversed Meaning: Oppression

The reversed Emperor is deliberating and stubborn. He is more interested in controlling than supporting you, and his love of convention here turns to oppression, overruling your needs or ideas. The reversed Emperor can therefore predict problems with parental or other authority figures, but be aware that this is not always a bad thing. Asserting your independence will also liberate you from guilt associated with the past.

Card Combinations

With the Magician, there is focused creativity as ideas take a workable form. With the Fool, a man with status brings adventure. With Strength comes gentle determination.

The Black Eagle and the Emperor

The imperial black eagle officially became an insignia of the Visconti family (see page 9) in 1397, two years after Gian Galeazzo Visconti had bought himself the hereditary title of Duke of Milan. Gian Galeazzo had deposed his uncle Bernabo in 1385 to take power, and the family's prominence grew as it ruled over much of northern Italy. In 1395, Gian Galeazzo purchased his title from Emperor Wenceslas of Germany. The newly created dukedom formed a part of the Roman Empire, which granted the use of the black eagle to the Viscontis. In the Visconti-Sforza Tarot, the Emperor wears the symbol of the black eagle on his hat; the card may therefore represent Emperor Wenceslas, although there are numerous theories regarding his original identity. In the Ancient Italian Tarot (1880), the eagle appears as an emblem on the Empress' shield, whereas on the Emperor card the eagle is a living creature, poised to protect the domain of the Emperor, who rests his left arm on the creature's head, emphasizing greater male, and specifically paternal, power. In shamanic cultures, the eagle is a symbol of the father.

V The Hierophant

The High Priest, The Pope

The Hierophant's obvious counterpart is card II, the High Priestess. However, he can be seen more keenly as the successor of card IV, the Emperor. In the Hierophant, he graduates from his earthly boundaries to the spiritual plane. The law of the land is transformed into the limitless possibilities available through education. The Hierophant may appear as an orthodox Catholic, but in a reading, he represents the nature of our individual faith.

Symbolism

The Hierophant's headdress is the triple crown which, with his crook or scepter, expresses his religious authority. With one hand, he makes the sign of giving a blessing. His throne is white, symbolizing purity. Like the High Priestess, he is seated between two pillars indicating his knowledge; yet his wisdom, unlike her hidden learning, is openly dispensed. In the Grigonneur (Charles VI) cards, and many other early decks, the Hierophant is identified as the Pope. He is depicted with two cardinals; he is a teacher who strives for unity between the mundane and the spiritual realms. Numbered V, the number of mankind, the Hierophant arbitrates the relationship between man and god. Five also represents the idea of unity.

Astrology

The sign associated with the Hierophant or Pope is Taurus, whose symbol is the Bull. A papal law or edict may also be referred to as a papal bull.

Upright Meaning: Education

In the upright position, the Hierophant foretells teaching, spiritual advancement, and the sense of freedom that progress brings. Divine inspiration is available to you—in the detail of everyday life, in the order of nature that is universally shared. This card shows you the sanctuary of a community, particularly in relation to education, such as a study group, which supports and encourages your learning. For individuals, the Hierophant can take the form of a teacher-angel who watches over you from above. In some instances, the Hierophant's association with unity can also predict a partnership or marriage.

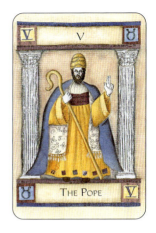

Reversed Meaning: Restriction

When the Hierophant is in the reversed position, misinformation or a drive for unreasonable or unattainable perfection is revealed. Restrictive attitudes and the lack of a free flow of ideas casts suspicion and creates an atmosphere of mistrust. The Hierophant reversed can therefore manifest as an organizational crisis at work or, for individuals, as self-criticism that blocks projects. During this confusing influence, make a vow to motivate yourself with achievable goals that you alone appreciate and define.

Card Combinations

It can be helpful to think of the Hierophant as a symbol of tradition, as well as learning. As with the Emperor, he can also represent a parent. Compare his qualities with those of the other cards that surround him.

The Hierophant with
the Ten of Wands
An educational commitment brings
a heavy workload

The Hierophant with
the Lovers
A partnership, possibly marriage,
which involves co-working

VI The Lovers

The Lovers represents a meeting of two hearts. However, it also reveals a landmark decision about love that requires risk and maturity. There are two conflicting paths that mark this rite of passage; a readiness to take risks and maturity are needed if the right choice is to be made. This is a stage in one's life that is ultimately about growing up, moving from the family toward establishing an independent life. In modern psychology this can be expressed as choosing a partner over one's mother or father.

Symbolism

Red roses and flowers surround both lovers, who meet each other on equal terms. The blooms together with the card number, VI, represent growth. In the Visconti-Sforza deck, the two figures have been identified by Tarot scholars as Bianca Maria Visconti and Francesco Sforza. Their marriage in 1441 was commemorated by the commissioning of the Visconti-Sforza Tarot (see page 9). The robes of both figures are decorated with suns surrounded by wavy and straight rays, which were heraldic devices of the Visconti-Sforza family. Cupid appears above the couple on a fountain, poised to release his arrow.

THE LOVERS AND
THE ACE OF CUPS
Falling in love; marriage,
pregnancy

Astrology

The sign of the Lovers is Gemini, the Twins. As the twins gaze at each other in union, so too they can turn away from commitment.

Upright Meaning: The Flower of Love

An opportunity to move on, but in order to do so an essential decision needs to be made. This often concerns the past and the future, in terms of letting go of one life phase to welcome the new. In families, this may concern duty to a relative that compromises a relationship. When this card appears in a reading you go for what you want and consequently energy and vision are your rewards. In this sense, the Lovers is about commitment to love itself and for yourself, not just love for an individual.

Reversed Meaning: Non-commitment

When the Lovers invert, you go for the easy option, the path of least resistance, which gets you out of a troublesome situation. This, however, is temporary and takes you no further forward in your relationships or in terms of self-confidence. Another meaning of this card is temptation and possible betrayal, in the sense that you undervalue your needs; this card may also reveal an emotional betrayal by a partner, but more often a failure of nerve to make a mature decision.

Card Combinations

When surrounded by positive cards, the Lovers reveals that you make the right decision regarding a relationship. When negative cards are close by, you take the path of least resistance that leaves important issues unresolved.

The Lovers and the Devil	The Lovers and the Chariot
A love decision that leads to entrapment or lack of fulfillment	A positive choice bringing travel and a new way of life

VII The Chariot

The charioteer, like the Hermit, is a mystic crusader who must manage many aspects of his life and psyche in order to ensure his progress. With the previous card, the Lovers, a decision was made; the Chariot can therefore be interpreted as the resulting action of a positive choice. Life drives forward, and the charioteer must show steady purpose if he is to gain the valuable experience that his journey offers. He can be likened to the Roman charioteer who parades in victory; however, in his triumph he must also rein in his ego.

Symbolism

The charioteer is male in many decks, but the Visconti-Sforza deck depicts a woman at the reins, dressed in similar style to that of the female lover on card VI; she may therefore represent Bianca-Maria Visconti (see page 9). The horses symbolize libido and desire, which he or she must learn to listen to and harness; if the horses run wild, the charioteer loses balance. The colors of the horses, which in later decks tend to be black and white, signify the dark and light aspects of the journey. The little moons on the charioteer's armor in the Rider Waite deck associate him with the Moon and therefore emotion. Numbered VII, this card combines the action of three with the stability of four, which represents moving onward from a strong position; VII may also represent the sum of the four-wheeled chariot, two horses, and charioteer.

Astrology

The Chariot is associated with emotional Cancer, the Crab. Like the Crab with his hard shell and soft center, he must balance his head and heart in order to move forward.

Upright Meaning: Determination

Keep going; you are in greater control of your life than you imagine. This card reveals that you are showing a determined effort to make progress. This is a long journey, but here—as with the Hermit—it is the journey, and not the quality of the destination, that is highlighted. This is a tremendous opportunity to learn as you experience, to respond and act at every stage. You are giving yourself a true education, but remember to appreciate the gifts that you gain. On a more mundane level, the Chariot can signify driving a car or purchasing a new vehicle.

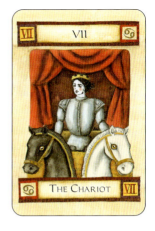

Reversed Meaning: Frustration

Ego or emotion is overtaking you; this may be a reflection of your attitude, or a sign of imbalance in those upon whom you depend. The Chariot reversed brings an arrogant charioteer, expecting unqualified support from those around him. On a practical level, the upturned Chariot reveals delayed travel and unexpected obstacles barring your path. This misdirection of well-intentioned plans may lead you to believe that you have taken the wrong route in life. One way to get through the influence of this card is to look at the areas of life that you have neglected and to switch your focus. Concentrate on small, achievable tasks, whether domestic or financial; displacement activity is better than waiting around doing little but berating your circumstances.

Card Combinations

With Justice, a journey is morally justified; an outcome in your favor brings freedom. With Judgment, an era is near its end, and a new phase in life beckons.

The Chariot as the Persona

In kabbala, each Tarot trump has an associated Hebrew letter and a correspondence on the Tree of Life (see page 26). In this system, the Chariot takes the letter heth, or chet, meaning fence or enclosure. This enclosure is the chariot itself, which is a metaphor for the shell of the personality that protects our vulnerability. However, at some point the shell can become restrictive and must be expanded or discarded, just as the developing personality must adapt to fit one's circumstances. In this sense, the charioteer's challenge is growth and movement that is consistent with his purpose.

VIII
JUSTICE

THE SCALES

The Justice card literally stands for justice: it reveals fairness, logic, and legal decisions that are generally favorable. But there is also an element of retribution in this card, so it may bring the righting of previous wrongs and the restoration of balance. The sword brandished by Justice, like the suit of Swords of the minor arcana, implies the wielding of reason rather than the flow of emotion.

SYMBOLISM

In classical art, Justice often appears blindfolded, displaying impartiality toward a defendant. In Tarot, Justice is not blindfolded because here we are concerned with the more subtle issues of the judicial process—moral fairness, emotional contracts, spiritual summings up—and we need to see these clearly in order to learn. On the Visconti-Sforza card, a knight on a white steed appears to fly over the central figure; knights bring speed and action, the effect of the enactment of Justice. Justice also resembles the female on the Lovers, the Chariot, and the four Queens, so she may represent Bianca-Maria Sforza (see page 78). Justice is usually numbered VIII (or XI, depending on the deck), which evokes absolute balance, comprising two stable fours. She carries the traditional objects of her craft, the scales and sword.

ASTROLOGY

Justice is associated with Libra, the Scales. The Scales represent evaluation, fairness, and balance.

Where Did Chastity Go?

Justice is one of the cardinal virtues, along with Temperance, Fortitude (Strength), Prudence, and Chastity. Justice, Temperance, and Strength survive in modern Tarots; Prudence existed in earlier decks, such as the Italian *tarocchi* of Mantegna (c. 1470) and the late eighteenth-century French Etteilla Tarot. However, there is little historical evidence of Chastity in the major arcana. So what happened to her, if indeed she existed?

In theology, Chastity may be expressed through the virtue of Charity. As Charity is about loving others, Chastity can be defined as giving love appropriately. As one of the Pauline virtues, Charity was depicted with Faith and Hope in the Cary-Yale Visconti-Sforza Tarot. The female figure on this Charity card holds a child and wears an ermine-trimmed robe. The ermine was a symbol of chastity because, in folklore, the animal would perish if its coat was sullied. A more obvious solution to the omission of Chastity from the Tarot may be found in the Catholic catechism, which states: "The virtue of chastity comes under the cardinal virtue of *temperance*, which seeks to permeate the passions and appetites of the senses with reason."

Upright Meaning: Resolution

A legal matter is resolved in fairness. This is justice in its truest sense, because it takes no heed of your position. Therefore, the appearance of Justice may be a card of satisfaction or discomfort, depending on your circumstances; the truth is that a final decision is made that must be accepted. Taken positively, Justice in the upright position legitimizes an endeavor and predicts success in business and legal dealings.

Reversed Meaning: Injustice

When reversed, Justice becomes a miscarriage of justice. You will know that you are right, yet the legal system goes against you. What you believe to be the truth is manipulated by others who are less qualified to fight your case. Fend off others' lack of faith and protect your integrity; choose new representatives or partners in business. Do not fall into the trap of punishing yourself unduly; one bad judgment is enough.

Card Combinations

Justice with Judgment reveals the practical and spiritual end of a situation. With the Wheel of Fortune, a summing-up leaves you free to experience greater opportunities.

IX The Hermit

Time

The Hermit reveals a time to be alone. Often depicted wearing the habit of a monk, he chooses a lone path away from familiar comfort in order to pursue a personal quest. He is solitary rather than lonely, as his moving away from society is chosen by him. He embraces nature as a way to heal himself and is guided by the light of his inner strength. When he appears in a reading, he brings a quieter pace of life; time slows down.

Symbolism

The Hermit's lit lantern represents inner guidance and truth. In some decks, such as the Visconti-Sforza, the Hermit holds an hourglass, a reference to his secondary title of Time. His snake-encircled staff symbolizes the caduceus, the emblem associated with Asclepius, the ancient Greeks' god of healing. The dark path shows the solitariness of the Hermit's spiritual journey on his quest for inner truth. His number, IX, may symbolize truth in Hebrew. The number nine comprises three triads, representing the integration of mind, body, and spirit. Nine also implies values—the Nines in the minor arcana (see page 137) are known as the ultimates of their suits.

The Hermit with the Star	The Hermit with Death
A time of withdrawal that leads to inspiration and creativity	A new way of thinking; a quiet positive time after the trauma of change

THE MAJOR ARCANA

Astrology

The Hermit's sign is Virgo, the Virgin. In this sense the Hermit is linked with card II, the High Priestess, who also seeks and holds knowledge that is hidden.

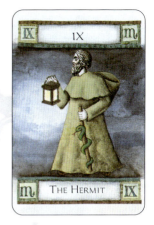

Upright Meaning: The Journey

The Hermit can reveal a need for recuperation and healing. You have to rely upon yourself, but you have the resourcefulness and integrity to find your way, symbolized by the Hermit's lantern. This is an important card for self-knowledge and inner strength. It can also reveal a physical journey that will bring emotional reward, but is often seen as a state of mind rather than actually going on a spiritual retreat. The appearance of the Hermit in a reading also relates to needing more time—to go at a pace that allows you to think clearly.

Reversed Meaning: Isolation

The Hermit reversed reveals isolation that is imposed rather than chosen. You may be cut off from your usual support systems or feel cast out by a community; in this context, the lone hermit is sad and world-weary. This is circumstantial, however, and the isolation temporary. Bear in mind that this card can also be a reflection of your fear of being rejected by others. As the upright Hermit needs time to consider and reflect, so in the reversed position there is intransigence. Stubbornness or rash reactions, rather than thought, see this hermit lose his way in the wilderness.

Card Combinations

When interpreting the Hermit with other cards, you may like to consider issues of time. With the Hermit, time slows down, whereas the Aces and Knights of the more physically active suits (Pentacles and Swords) generally show that events will speed up. For example, the Hermit combined with the Knight of Pentacles would reveal a time of rest followed by intense activity.

The Hermit with
the Ace of Pentacles
Renewed energy; successfully resuming
practical affairs after a time of healing

X The Wheel of Fortune

Fate

The Wheel of Fortune marks the halfway stage in the cycle of the major arcana. After the contemplative Hermit card, with the Wheel comes the darker side of nature: the unconscious. We get to know ourselves better. This card's secondary title, Fate, illustrates its literal meaning. To rail against Fate is pointless, and we can only go with its flow. In Buddhism, this may be thought of as an understanding of non-attachment: we may explore our own psyches, but we cannot control the greater workings of the universe.

Symbolism

The Visconti-Sforza deck shows a wheel with the figure of Fortune. Surrounding her are four figures that represent aspects of fate. Many later decks portray animals representing the cycle of death and rebirth. The monkey is vanity, impermanence; the ass is humility and human error; the dragon is the primal energy of nature. The dragon brandishes a sword, like the figure of Justice, card VIII. Like the Egyptian deity Osiris, the dragon is the guardian of the underworld. With the turning of the wheel, we need to be ready to see and experience life from all sides. The wheel symbolizes the rotating of fortune and the seasons. In Buddhism, the wheel is a symbol of *dharma*, the Buddha's teachings. This card is numbered X, which signifies completeness.

Astrology

The Wheel of Fortune card is associated with Jupiter, the planet linked with luck and learning.

Upright Meaning: The Unexpected

The Wheel heralds a change in fortune. Be open to change; as you seek and gain new knowledge, so you can accept whatever life throws at you. Spiritually, this card can reveal that there's a whole side of life you haven't seen before. It can represent meeting your unconscious self, which may be a darker aspect of your personality or desires that you usually keep hidden. However, its normal meaning is positive: anything is possible.

Reversed Meaning: Closure

Unlike many major arcana cards, the reversed Wheel is not negative. The natural order and disorder of the universe may be beyond your control, but the focus is on how you experience the changes of fortune that it brings about. You may have difficulty adapting if you feel that the wheel has turned against you, but it is important to accept your situation, rather than rail against perceived injustice. Thankfully, the Wheel reversed also foretells closure, the ending of one cycle of destiny. This may bring you welcome relief.

Card Combinations

Like the Death card, the Wheel of Fortune indicates a level of immediate change, usually for the better. The cards that follow the Wheel reveal in which areas of the querent's life this turn of events will be most keenly felt.

The Wheel of Fortune with the Moon (*Right*)
A twist of fate brings about a crisis of confidence; an inability to accept one's circumstances

The Wheel of Fortune with Judgment (*Left*)
Events that accidentally work in your favor; synchronicity that quickly concludes important business

XI
Strength

Fortitude

Along with Justice and Temperance, Strength (or Fortitude) is the second of the cardinal virtues to appear in the major arcana sequence (see page 63). The nature of Strength is illuminated here; it is not the brute force that tames the lion, but patience and gentleness. Strength can point to an internal conflict rather than an external enemy. This calls for strength of character, a need to integrate the base and higher aspects of our personalities.

Symbolism

The lion symbolizes primal instinct that has to be tamed. In the Visconti-Sforza deck, a muscular figure wields a club against the cowed animal. He uses a club rather than a sword, perhaps aiming to subdue the lion rather than kill it. The lion here has an almost human face; Strength is also concerned with taming one's own baser nature. In later decks such as the Rider Waite, the lion contrasts with the gentrified, clothed lady, who represents civilized society. Her hat makes the shape of a lazy eight, the lemniscate, which is also the Magician's insignia (see page 68); it symbolizes infinity. The card number, XI indicates tension. One beyond the even ten, it denotes excess and imbalance. Adding together the individual numbers: one plus one gives two; in Tarot, the Twos (see page 116) indicate a struggle for balance, rather than assumed balance or equality.

Astrology

Strength is associated with Leo, the Lion. In alchemy, the lion is a symbol of primary matter that can be transformed into gold, a euphemism for an enlightened state of mind.

Upright Meaning: Tension

When upright, this card signifies inner strength and patience to deal with passionate forces that may be overwhelming. These may be external or within yourself—the lion can reveal that you are fighting your own shadow. Taming the lion, however, is not about takeover—more about gentle persuasion and a degree of courage when facing a potentially dangerous opponent. In a reading, Strength shows how to deal with a difficult situation or person whose outlook is very different from your own. It also reveals the need for feminine and masculine qualities to come together for balance. Patience, not force, is the solution. This card can also signify good health and abundant energy.

Reversed Meaning: Avoidable Danger

The negative in this card is not the lion, but a fear of the lion. Strength reversed is a weakness of will and an inability to take a genuine risk; rather than deal with discomfiting tension as you work out how to resolve a conflict, you try to deny the enemy all together. This may be the enemy within: when you don't want to listen to your gut instinct for fear of what action you may need to take. The message here is not to panic, and to recognize that you need only compromise a little to win your case.

Card Combinations

The Strength card is advice in itself, but when combined with other cards, it enables you to discover more about the nature of a test: this may be a test of will, a moral question, or inner conflict with your conscience or with your head and heart.

STRENGTH WITH THE HANGED MAN
An ongoing test of will that leads to a sacrifice or change of mind

STRENGTH WITH THE FOOL
An attempt to resolve an issue, opting for escape rather than resolution

XII The Hanged Man

The Traitor

The Hanged Man may initially appear to be a card of punishment. However, his experience leads him to a new truth because now he can see life from an altered perspective. Hanging from a tree, he is reminiscent of Odin, the Norse god who discovered the secrets of the Norse runes by suspending himself from the World Tree for nine nights. The Hanged Man's peaceful expression reveals his confidence in his predicament. He is safely held while he takes time to see the world from another angle.

Symbolism

The tree is the Tree of Life, which is central to kabbala (see page 24). The protective garland of leaves that encircles him is open-ended, which indicates that he still has much to accomplish on his journey through the major arcana; the full circle, symbolizing completion, is depicted as a garland on the World, the final card of beginnings and endings (see page 108). The Hanged Man's left foot is safely tethered to the branch of the tree, which shows that the universe will support him. He does not need to cling to the tree, but simply to await the insights that his stance will afford him. The Hanged Man is numbered XII, which represents salvation.

Astrology

The Hanged Man is associated with the element of Water and the planet Neptune. Neptune is the planet of fantasy and the imagination. Water relates to the emotions.

Upright Meaning: A Change of Perspective

The Hanged Man reveals the need to look at life from a different perspective, to step away from immediate problems. There is no sense of death here, only that you may need to muster your strength to discard a dream—if your new-found view on the situation requires it. Tarotist Alfred Douglas writes that the Hanged Man reveals a reversal of values; in this way, an unorthodox solution to a problem may present itself. On a practical level, this card reveals that you must be patient as you hang about awaiting the outcome of an important decision.

Reversed Meaning: A Waste of Time

You may think that you are tied to one course of action, but this is just an excuse for inaction. Guidance from your unconscious and an openness to look at alternatives will liberate you from indecision—an unrealistic fantasy will only bind you faster. Release yourself from a contract with others or with yourself that cannot be fulfilled.

Card Combinations

With the Hermit, time out for study or self-examination is revealed. With Death, discarding some dreams may lead to the natural ending of a way of living.

The Identity of the Hanged Man

An alternative name for the Hanged Man is the Traitor, which is the title of the card in Etteilla decks. The Hanged Man in the Visconti-Sforza Tarot may portray Muzio Attendolo, an Italian *condottiere* or mercenary who was famous in the late fourteenth century. During the Hundred Years War, Attendolo rose to fame when his band of mercenaries helped Gian Galeazzo Visconti to defeat the Della Scala family in 1387. For his heroism he was dubbed *sforza*, or "strength"; in 1424 this title was granted to him as a hereditary surname. Attendolo killed the tyrant Ottobuono Terzo, an enemy of the Pope, but trouble came when he complained that Pope John had not paid him for services rendered, and changed sides to fight for King Ladislaus of Naples. According to the scholar Geoffrey Trease, the Pope was so angered by Sforza's defection that he commissioned a satirical illustration showing him as a traitorous hanged man.

XIII
Death

The Skeleton

In many Tarot decks, Death is depicted as the Grim Reaper, shrouded or unshrouded, and in some packs as an animated ghoul. Yet the true meaning of this card is rarely physical death—Death heralds the end of an era, which usually comes as a relief rather than a trauma. This is winter time, when older values are replaced by budding ideas. This card signifies the walk between the old and the new, and is auspicious for the fresh beginnings that are expressed in card 0, the Fool, and card I, the Magician.

Symbolism

In the Visconti-Sforza deck, Death is a skeleton-archer who holds what appears to be vertebrae or a snakelike rope in his left hand, and sometimes a slim arrow in his right. It is likely that the vertebrae are part of a bow; like Cupid (and like love itself), Death strikes at random. While traditional Tarots show Death as a skeleton or Grim Reaper, there are other interpretations, one of which is shown opposite. Here, the sun is going down on an old way of living, and dead trees recede to make way for the new. The number of the card is XIII, today still thought of as an unlucky number. Its sum is four (three plus one), which has connotations of death in Chinese numerology. In Western tradition, however, four is the number of stability, representing the aftermath and return to order that follows the emotional chaos of bereavement. On the Rider Waite Death card, the skeleton on horseback holds a banner that bears the symbol of the rose, which symbolizes renewal.

Astrology

Death is associated with Scorpio, the Scorpion. Scorpio is linked with sex and death, the ultimate in beginnings and endings—the dual message of the Death card.

Upright Meaning: Natural endings

The natural ending of one cycle of destiny; a moving away from old familiar patterns toward new opportunities. This represents a major life change that you will welcome, not fear. It may appear in readings to signify relocation to a new home or job, or the final ending of a relationship that you have outgrown, with the knowledge that fresh potential lies just around the corner. Remember that this symbolic death is necessary to enable you to move on, and is not about grief or regret; it is simply a natural progression for you at this point in your life.

Reversed Meaning: Unexpected Change

Death reversed may occur in a reading to show you that it is time to let go. You may have been holding on to outdated information or a relationship that you are continuing for the sake of it, although it is not fulfilling. If you cannot make the decision right now, this card indicates that change may be made for you. In this sense, Death reversed reveals unexpected events occurring : take this card as an opportunity to prepare yourself.

Card Combinations

At its simplest level, Death shows change, so the surrounding cards help illuminate the nature of that change. It can be easier to read the second card first, then interpret the Death card, because the second card often reveals the impact of change and therefore the natural reason why a situation had to end.

Death with the Hierophant *(Right)*
A spiritual beginning; the comfort of religion during a time of chaos

Death with the Lovers *(Left)*
Leaving an established relationship or lifestyle for a new passion

XIV
Temperance

Temperance is the third cardinal virtue in the major arcana sequence, after Justice and Strength (see pages 82, 88). A maiden or an angel pours water from one cup or urn to another. She is a spiritual alchemist, integrating and harmonizing the varied essences of life. The meaning of Temperance is the advent of a practical test in which we manage the demands on our time. Equally, she heralds the need to balance complementary and conflicting aspects of our personality.

Symbolism

The angel or maiden on the card is the Angel of Time, who presides over the past and the future and through whom emotions flow, symbolized by the water. On some decks, the angel has one foot in the pool, the other on land. This represents a striving for balance by careful management of temperamental factors. The irises growing by the water are named after Iris, the Greek rainbow-goddess who brought messages to Earth from the sky-god, Zeus. Her symbol is the rainbow, a symbol of hope that appears on decks such as the Crystal Tarot. The number of Temperance is XIV, for reconciliation and growth.

Astrology

Temperance is associated with Sagittarius, the Archer or Centaur. The glyph for Sagittarius is the arrow. On the Temperance card, water from the higher urn must be poured at a precise angle to fill the lower; in the same way must the archer have true aim.

Upright Meaning: Reconciliation

You may need to approach a challenging situation with scientific precision. It takes concentration to get the formula right if you are to attain a harmonious balance. Although life feels like a continual balancing act with all its demands on your time, believe in your ability to judge a situation adeptly. Success, however, requires commitment and effort. The card also suggests reconciliation, and the resolution of issues from the past in order to create the future you desire.

Reversed Meaning: Imbalance

Temperance reversed indicates a tidal wave of trouble. This manifests as imbalance—past events threaten to overwhelm you as your usual focus on the present dissolves. This card can also signify poor financial management or a general lack of resources. In love, difficult memories may surface, which may restrict a current relationship. Attention to detail is the best way out of the whirlpool; you are dealing with sensitive issues.

Card Combinations

With the Four of Swords, a welcome rest after a stressful time is revealed. With the World, hard work brings deserved reward.

Angels in Time

Traditionally, angels appear on the Judgment and Temperance cards. On the latter, the angel has been identified as the archangel Michael, who rules the Sun. On the Judgment card, the angel is the archangel Gabriel, ruler of the element of Water. This element is therefore associated with both cards. As the flow of water can represent the past progressing to the future, angels and water together speak of purification and regeneration. Water itself brings life, and is used to symbolize renewal and energy in rituals ranging from Christian baptism to the water-blessings of charity *jambhalas* in Buddhism. The angels are Angels of Time: on the Judgment card, the angel calls that it is time to begin again; on Temperance, that it is time for reconciliation.

XV The Devil

Tarot cards traditionally depict the Devil card as Satan enslaving a male and female demon. One origin of the Devil is Pan, who was the Greek god of excess (rather than evil). It is important to recognize that the message of this card is illusion and extremes; the only dark forces are those of our own making. When the Devil appears, a decision must be made between our base instincts—fear, lust, greed—and our higher natures.

Symbolism

In the Visconti-Sforza Tarot, the Devil is a horned and winged beast who holds two naked figures in his mouth—one male, one female—as if to devour them. His hind legs appear to be reversed; the human face depicted below the Devil's head symbolizes the human face of suffering. A modern interpretation is shown on page 97, top left: a central figure appears with an angel of conscience on one shoulder and a devil of temptation on the other. Both are figments of the imagination, and reveal the Devil's meaning as the conflict of opposing internal forces. In the Rider Waite deck, an inverted pentagram appears, which is sometimes thought of as a representation of the Devil's head; his beard is the lowest point of the pentagram, with his ears and horns associated with the middle and upper pairs of points that constitute the form. His number is XV, which in numerology reduces to six: five plus one. This is the number of the Lovers, which also shows two figures and reveals that a vital choice must be made.

The Devil with the Six of Cups
A choice between love and security
or eroticism and excitement

THE MAJOR ARCANA

Astrology

The Devil's astrological sign is Capricorn, the Goat. The Goat is associated with goat-headed Pan, the Roman god of excess. Many depictions of the Devil on Tarot cards are a likeness of Pan.

Upright Meaning: Obligation

Guilt or fear holds you to an unsatisfactory obligation. You may believe that there is no way out of an addictive affair, a moral debt, or employment with little reward. This, however, is merely your perception, not the reality. At any point, you can choose to walk away; it is, after all, a situation that you alone have created. The Devil urges you to make a mature choice that will bring long-term benefits to your life, rather than short-term gratification.

Reversed Meaning: Enslavement

The upright meaning of the Devil is intensified in the reversed position. Here, the sense of temptation is acute. Something or someone you desire exacts a high price—but only if you give in. The chaotic Devil may manifest as others attempting to manipulate your better side; ask for a little angelic intervention, and resist.

Card Combinations

The cards placed around the Devil help reveal the nature of hidden energies around us. The second card can provide more information about the kind of temptation that the querent may be dealing with, or what may strengthen his or her resolve when life is generally difficult.

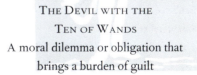

The Devil with the Ace of Pentacles reversed	The Devil with the Ten of Wands
The temptation of money; corruption	A moral dilemma or obligation that brings a burden of guilt

XVI
THE TOWER

THE HOUSE OF GOD

The Tower means unavoidable disaster: literally, an act of God as implied by the card's alternative title, the House of God or *La Maison Dieu*. Like the arrow of love from Cupid or the scythe of Death, lightning can strike at any time. However, with ultimate destruction a new path is cleared for regeneration. In classical myth, a flash of lightning emitted by Zeus impregnated Semele, Princess of Thebes, with her son Dionysos. Dionysos was the god of wine, and he is therefore associated with altered states—the aftershock that the Tower represents.

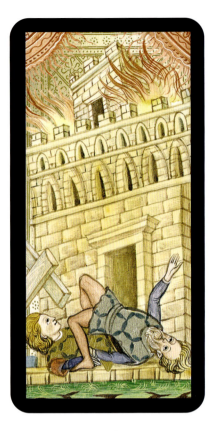

SYMBOLISM

The Tower can be seen as the Tower of Babel destroyed by God; the lightning striking the Tower represents divine retribution, and the fire symbolizes purification, which sparks a new beginning. In the Visconti-Sforza deck, intense rays of the sun appear to inflame the tower, and a cross falls with the two male figures. The cross symbolizes resurrection: the figures appear temporarily immobilized rather than dead, as if waiting to be reanimated. The falling figures on Tower Tarot cards represent the fallout—emotional, physical, and spiritual—that comes with disaster. The card is numbered XVI, for the cosmic power of the elements.

ASTROLOGY

The Tower is associated with Mars, the fiery planet of war. Mars expresses the violent destruction and aftermath of release that the Tower may bring.

The Buddha and the Thunderbolt

In Buddhism, one of the sacred devotional objects is the *djore* (Tibet) or *vajra* (India), which means "thunderbolt." It represents the destruction of ignorance and the purification of the mind that is vital if one is to remove the imprint of the negative karma that we inherit at birth. The buddha of purification is Vajrasattva, a tantric deity who holds a *vajra* (or thunderbolt) in his right hand and a *ghanta* (or bell) for wisdom in the other. In Tantric ritual, the thunderbolt and bell are used together, so that their interaction signifies enlightenment. The *vajra* is also a symbol of the Hindu god Indra, king of heaven and god of rain, implying that a bolt of apparent destruction lights up the sky and the consciousness, so that purification—symbolized by water—can follow.

Upright Meaning: Disaster

The Tower represents sudden collapse. A bolt from the blue destroys what you have constructed: a lifestyle, business venture, relationship, or dream. On a psychological level, it reveals the temporary deconstruction of the self. This can result in a shattered ego: your defences are down and you are vulnerable. The Tower signifies a fall from grace and represents fate at work. It does not therefore suggest blame—only bad fortune that is unavoidable. In the aftermath, you can pick up the pieces and reclaim your ground. What you create now will have a stronger foundation than what you thought you had.

Reversed Meaning: Blame

The Tower reversed reveals disaster that may have been avoidable. You may have created a basis for instability in your life, and now what you feared most has happened: the collapse of your dreams and an apparent attack on your security. Just as the upright Tower represents painful but necessary destruction, so what you suffer here may seem unjust. Accept what has happened and analyze its cause. Letting go of blame will help you find a way to rebuild your confidence and move forward.

Card Combinations

With the Star, apparent misfortune ushers in a creative phase.
With the Three of Swords, a relationship suffers.

XVII
The Star

The appearance of the Star is a call from the cosmos, offering us inspiration and creativity. This is a card of growth and replenishment, symbolized by the actions of the central figure—often depicted as a naked woman—who returns half of her water to the pool and feeds the earth with the remaining water from the cup in her right hand. The gifts of the Star are insight and healing.

Symbolism

The Star and Temperance are similar in their composition, particularly in the Visconti-Sforza deck, as both show a lone female with a goblet in each hand. On the Temperance card, the two goblets must be held at an almost magical angle if the water is to flow; on the Star, however, the water flows plentifully. This represents a wave of creativity that comes as naturally as breathing. A harmonious balance between the unconscious and conscious mind is signified by equal water pouring into the pool (the unconscious) and on to the earth (consciousness). The Star's number is XVII; when reduced (one plus seven), this gives eight. In the Visconti-Sforza Tarot, a woman touches an eight-pointed star with her left hand. Eight stars are depicted on later decks, and the number is linked with renewal (see page 134). One star shines more brightly than the others; this is the guiding star, a powerful symbol of hope.

Astrology

The Star card is associated with Aquarius, the Water-carrier of the zodiac. Water and stars together represent healing and inspiration from the cosmos.

THE MAJOR ARCANA

Upright Meaning: Inspiration

The Star reveals healing and harmony that are both physical and spiritual. Inner desires, which take form through your dreams, can now be consciously expressed. This card is therefore fortuitous for artists and for entrepreneurs, but for everyone it is a sign of hope, energy, and boundless creativity. Reaching your true potential will bring freedom and inspiration that are truly divine.

Reversed Meaning: Creative Block

The Star reversed can reveal a creative block, as with the reversed Magician (see page 69). You may not be able to fulfill your dreams just now; as starlight is bewitching, so is an impossible fantasy. In this context, the practical details that make a project hold true are overlooked. While it is compelling to dream, be aware that you need to identify your real-life expectations. This applies too to a dreamer in your life, who may lull you into partaking in a venture that has no chance of success.

Card Combinations

A helpful reminder of the meaning of the Star in a reading is its star quality—it can show a major dream or need for the querent. The surrounding cards may reveal whether this dream complements or clashes with other major or minor events.

The Star with the Five of Coins *(Right)*
A lack of courage; fear that a dream come true will fail

The Star with the Devil *(Left)*
A conflict between freedom and restraint; a decision to take a higher path in life

XVIII
The Moon

The Moon reveals a crisis of faith. As moonlight makes the world look different, this card depicts the surfaces of the inner world or subconscious mind. Old or unresolved fears surface; the darker aspects of our personality, like the night wolves on modern tarot Moon cards, come out to play. This can result in a bewildering indecisiveness that may feel exhausting, leaving little energy with which to move forward. In reality, however, the crayfish does not have far to go if he chooses to stay in his natural habitat or take the risk of moving forward.

Symbolism

On the Visconti-Sforza card, a woman holds a broken bow, a symbol of failure. She may represent the huntress Diana, who cannot pursue her quarry. In modern decks such as the Rider Waite, two wolves howl by two towers; twin irises grow by a pool. The Twos symbolize tension and, here, a conflict of choice. With his body, the crayfish bridges a critical void between the unconscious and conscious mind. The water represents the inner emotions and the past; the dry land signifies the world beyond, which he must negotiate. The wolves symbolize instinct that cries for freedom. They are also fierce guardians, so the crayfish's journey—if he takes it—may involve a hazardous rite of passage. The crayfish represents the soul, and therefore our deepest yearnings. The Moon is numbered XVIII, which reduces to nine: eight plus one. In the minor arcana, Nines represent the ultimate values of their suits (see page 137). Here, the nine shows the ultimate confusion of moonlight.

Astrology

The Moon's astrological sign is Pisces, the Fish. The association of the Fish with the soul and the element of water in which he dwells—representing the emotions—indicates the intensity of feeling linked with the Moon card.

Upright Meaning: Disillusion

The Moon shows disillusionment on the surface, but beneath lies a greater emotional turmoil. As the crayfish does not know whether he should choose the safety of his habitat (the pool) or risk crawling on to dry land, so you may feel frustrated by choice, or simply paralyzed by the need to make a decision at all. However, expressing this paralysis through words can act as a first step toward a feeling of release. Rely on your instinct; this is unique to you, and will bring you much more than just survival.

Reversed Meaning: Avoidance

In the reversed position, the Moon reveals the danger of doing nothing. While this brings temporary respite, it cannot reward you with emotional resolution. In order to avoid the heat of a challenging or traumatic decision, you may be tempted to revise your expectations to fit what is on offer. However, burying your needs means that you may view others unrealistically, while continuing to deny yourself the opportunities you deserve.

Card Combinations

Helpful keywords when interpreting the Moon are illusion, disillusion, and confusion. This is an emotional card, so any card that follows the Moon in a reading can indicate how the querent deals with their emotions and moves forward.

The Moon with the World
Hesitation before the ending of a
phase; a need to let go
of the past

The Moon with the Sun
The ability to glimpse and achieve
success; a focus that will transcend a
time of self-questioning

THE MYSTERY OF THE TAROT

XIX
THE SUN

The Sun heralds a time of contentment, joy, and good health. Like the preceding cosmic cards, the Moon and the Star, the Sun reveals powerful energy at work. Its effect is a return to the optimism of childhood in an earthly paradise. The two children are a significant pairing, as Twos feature on many major arcana cards: the two cups of Temperance, the two demons under the yoke of the Devil, and the two Lovers. In these cards, the Twos can signify tension or decisions, but the Sun's two children are twinlike. Their similarity is harmonious, and they create an ambience of love and creativity.

SYMBOLISM

The Visconti-Sforza card depicts a cherub or winged boy, who holds a radiant sun with a human face. The child floats on a cloud over a fertile plain and blue mountains: with the sun in his hands, he carries the element of Fire. The cloud represents the elements of Air and Water, and the plain the Earth. All four elements are present to support his growth. Many decks show two children in a walled garden (see page 105, top right). The children signify energy and joy; the garden and the towering sunflowers represent growth and innocence. The wall is a metaphor for protection and the sense of emotional security that comes with life experience. In personality terms, the wall also symbolizes having appropriate boundaries. The sun signifies wholeness, and the children a coming together of the two parts of the self: the conscious and unconscious minds. The Sun's number, XIX, stands for achievement.

Astrology

The Sun's astrological association is with the planetary Sun. The Sun is concerned with the self, and brings renewal after the dark night of card XVIII, the Moon.

Upright Meaning: Success

The Sun is always a welcome card in a reading: its heat permeates all aspects of your life, bringing new relationships, children, health, happiness, and true success. In the early Grigonneur (Charles VI) deck, the Sun card depicts a woman spinning wool; this reveals that the threads of your life are coming together to create something that will warm you. This is also a time to take sanctuary in love, and to experience the pure joy of all that you have achieved.

Reversed Meaning: Delay

The Sun reversed shows that heat and light, the gifts of the upright Sun, are just out of reach. You can envisage a carefree existence without worries about health, children, and work; this may take the form of a holiday in the sun, or simply a time when you can expend energy on enjoying your relationships rather than solving problems. It is important to keep the faith rather than give up, as this card indicates delay, not defeat.

Card Combinations

Two keywords for the Sun are success and happiness. The cards that appear close to the Sun in a reading can show how a positive, productive phase is manifesting—in terms of relationships, finances, creativity, or simply recuperation.

<table>
<tr><td>

The Sun with the Ace of Wands
A venture that attracts practical support; ideas and conversations inspire creativity and new projects

</td><td>

The Sun with the Empress
A happy phase for a family in which success is shared; a new baby, a time of togetherness

</td></tr>
</table>

XX
Judgment

The Angel, The Trumpet, Fame

Judgment is the penultimate card in the major arcana cycle. It reveals the need for self-assessment before reaching card XXI, the World—which is concerned with completion and rebirth—and a return to card 0, the Fool. Judgment is a part of the renewal process, where we come to terms with the past before moving on. This card is a call to examine our previous actions. Rather than await the decree of others, as in card VIII, Justice, here a question is posed: how do you judge yourself?

Symbolism

The sword brandished by the authority figure on the Visconti-Sforza card echoes the sword held by Justice and by the dragon (or Fortuna) on the Wheel of Fortune. Here, it has a similar purpose in that it represents time to evaluate the past. The angels blow bannered trumpets: this is a wake-up call, a time to be counted by one's conscience rather than by the external world. Modern decks such as the Rider Waite often show water as part of the card imagery. This signifies *aqua libra*, the water of life that brings purification and regeneration. The water also symbolizes the subconscious, again reinforcing the play of conscience when assessing past actions and behavior. On the Visconti-Sforza card, three figures look upward from a tomb. The two children mirror the angels, and the old man the heavenly figure of Judgment above him. These are the earthly and spiritual sides of humans, indicating spiritual rebirth. The card is numbered XX, which reduces to two. This shows that we are close to integrating our conscious and unconscious selves; we are near to attaining the whole world.

Astrology

Judgment is associated with the element of Fire and the planet Pluto. Pluto is concerned with identity and a quest for truth. Pluto was the Roman god of the underworld (the Hades of Greek myth). He expresses the need to examine the darker side of our natures, the message of Judgment, before moving forward.

Acclaiming Trumpets

In Jewish tradition, trumpets were sounded to herald the beginning of a ten-day period, Rosh Hashanah, that ended with the Day of Atonement (Yom Kippur) or Last Judgment, marked by seven angels blowing seven trumpets. During this time one was expected to repent of one's sins and examine one's conscience: "Awake, ye sleepers from your sleep ... and ponder your deeds" (Numbers 29: 1). To Latter-day Saints, the Last Judgment is known as the Feast of Trumpets, when a fanfare will herald the Second Coming of Christ

The trumpet is associated with the onset of war, and with fame, because it announces royalty and those in the public eye. Tarotist Gertrude Moakley relates that the angel and trumpet reveal the triumph of fame; in some early *minchiate* Tarot decks, the Judgment card is also entitled "Fame." Perhaps this is the origin of "blowing your own trumpet," the self-acclamation that is often used to criticize boastfulness.

Upright Meaning: Renewal

An opportunity for renewal; a time of beginnings and endings during which you gain perspective on the past and look ahead to greater achievements. Judgment brings joy and reward for your work, rather than regret; you may look back, but with pleasure. This card can also indicate a second chance to do your duty, to take a fresh angle on an old situation, as well as an improvement in health. Whatever your situation, events will move quickly, as this card indicates a faster pace of life.

Reversed Meaning: Guilt

With Judgment in the reversed position, the chance to conclude a matter is delayed because you cannot confront your fear of change. This card can indicate that you feel guilty about the past, and therefore soul-searching holds you back. While it is appropriate to assess your morality, this can become so absorbing that you fail to notice what is going on in the present. Great opportunities may be missed if you don't let go. Pay attention to your immediate needs, and take care of your physical body too.

Card Combinations

Judgment with the High Priestess reveals that a situation is assessed intuitively rather than spoken aloud. Judgment with the Devil shows that it may be hard to move on and feel free in the world; you may need to make peace with yourself.

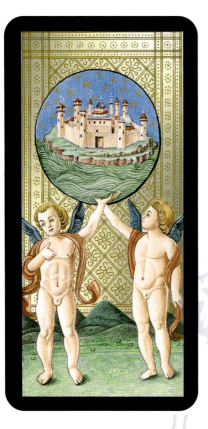

XXI The World

The Universe

The World, or Universe—the final card in the twenty-two-card sequence of the major arcana—represents successful completion. Along with the Sun, it is one of the most positive cards in a reading. It brings the respect and acknowledgment of those who have witnessed our efforts.

Symbolism

In the Visconti-Sforza deck, two cherubs hold a ring inside which is a walled city under a starry sky. This may symbolize a heavenly paradise, a perfect world. In the Marseilles and Rider Waite decks, the garland forms the almond shape of a *mandorla*, which is used in religious iconography to frame holy figures. The *mandorla* symbolizes heaven on Earth. It is also the cosmic egg, a universal symbol of creation that implies the triumph of order over chaos. The card is numbered XXI: two plus one gives three, the number of creation. The figure on the card appears to be both male and female. The hermaphroditic quality indicates the final integration of the unconscious and conscious, and the harmonious balance between humans and the greater universe.

Astrology

The World is associated with the planet Saturn, the astrological taskmaster. Saturn is concerned with objectivity and duty, and working within recognized boundaries. The World card shows that you have completed your work in a way that others can recognize and reward.

Upright Meaning: Reward

The upright World card reveals success and a special reward. One part of your life is reaching a natural conclusion, and you are primed with energy and optimism about the future. It is time to take an essential step into the wider world. This can be expressed through the opportunity to explore literally by traveling, or by embarking on a new profession. Your lifestyle will change, as from now on you move to even greater success and enjoy a lifestyle that embraces all that you desire.

Reversed Meaning: Dilution

The card in this position shows outdated values, and a lack of determination to move toward positive change. Consequently, you are moving in ever-decreasing circles. The universe feels like a smaller place when you are stuck in an emotional deadlock. As with Judgment reversed, you can miss out on immediate offers because you are unable to direct your energies to the present moment. This may be due to painful past issues, but there comes a time to pull away from familiar patterns; even unhappiness can become comfortable over time, because you get so used to managing it. Break away, rather that lose out on what the rest of the world has to offer.

Card Combinations

When interpreting the World, consider that the card contains both beginnings and endings: in a reading, it can show that a new phase is already starting, so the cards that follow may reveal how the querent will proceed and what their journey will bring.

The World with the Fool *(Right)*
The start of an inspiring and successful phase that brings excitement and travel

The World with Justice *(Left)*
A decision in one's favor brings satisfaction and the freedom to start again

The Minor Arcana

THE MINOR ARCANA COMPRISES fifty-six cards that fall into four suits: Cups, Pentacles, Wands, and Swords. Each suit has ten numbered or "pip" cards, from the Ace through Ten, and four people or Court cards: the Page, Knight, Queen, and King. Until the early 1900s, the minor arcana pip cards showed geometric patterns to denote their number: two swords, three cups, or ten pentacles, for example. For a novice reader, there was no evocative imagery with which to play detective; if you were unfamiliar with the numerological value of a card or element of a suit, there was little else to guide you.

This changed in 1909 with the publication of the Rider Waite deck. For the first time, the meanings of the minor arcana were illuminated with fully illustrated pip cards. The artist was Pamela Colman Smith (1878–1951), whose graphic style was to inspire a host of modern decks, such as the Mystic Tarot (1975), Morgan Greer (1979), and Sheridan/Douglas Tarot (1972). The Universal Waite and Golden Waite decks use the line art of the original, but with revised colorings. The following pages show some Rider Waite examples.

Using Elements and Numbers

The Court cards can be notoriously difficult to interpret, because they are often thought to refer to individuals. If the interpretation of a Court card doesn't identify someone you know (for cards in past and present positions in a spread), then you have no other way to access an alternative meaning for the card. The way to deal with this is to think of the Court cards as broader energies, as well as significant people. To help you do this, the cards have been grouped by number or type: so all

ABOVE: *The Five of Pentacles (Coins) of the Rider Waite deck illustrates its literal meaning: feeling impoverished, excluded from comfort, and out in the cold.*

THE MINOR ARCANA

ABOVE: *The Ace of Cups from the Tarot of Marseilles. The ornate chalice has eight sides like a baptismal font, symbolizing the idea of renewal and regeneration.*

the Aces, Tens, and Queens, for instance, appear together. Each card group has its own introduction, which explains the meaning of that group's elements and number. Familiarizing yourself with these will give you more interpretative options, and in time you can be less reliant on referring to this book or any other instruction manual as you read the cards. In the Court card interpretations, the elemental associations that appear below the card title are those devised by the Order of the Golden Dawn (see page 18).

THE ROMANY METHOD

The Romany method interprets the Court cards as people; this technique was also used to read playing cards. It assigns each Court card with very basic physical attributes and status. While it gives too little information on its own, it can be a helpful addition when used in conjunction with more detailed character interpretations or element/number associations.

KINGS: Mature men with status
QUEENS: Mature women
KNIGHTS: Young men
PAGES: Teenagers and children of both genders

WANDS: Brown hair, pale skin
CUPS: Fair hair, pale skin
SWORDS: Dark hair, midtone skin
PENTACLES: Dark skin; short in height

INTERPRETING CARD PATTERNS

Another technique when reading the minor arcana is to look at the pattern of the cards before you. Assess the frequency of a suit's appearance: a spread laden with Pentacles, for example, indicates the querent's practical concern with money, security, and property. A prevalence of Cups indicates that relationships and emotions dominate. Naturally, this is a generalization, but it acts as a helpful starting point.

Some specific meanings have been attributed to patterns of cards. The esotericist A. E. Waite, a prominent member of the Order of the Golden Dawn, includes a list of possible meanings in his book *The Pictorial Key to the Tarot*. The list on page 112 has been adapted from his original.

THE KINGS
FOUR KINGS: acknowledgment, acclaim
THREE KINGS: consultation, advice
TWO KINGS: minor counsel

THE QUEENS
FOUR QUEENS: great debate
THREE QUEENS: friendship
TWO QUEENS: tension, rivalry

THE KNIGHTS
FOUR KNIGHTS: important events, sudden travel
THREE KNIGHTS: lively discussion
TWO KNIGHTS: reunions, intimacy

THE PAGES
FOUR PAGES: a gathering of young people
THREE PAGES: sociability
TWO PAGES: disquiet, annoyance

THE TENS
FOUR TENS: momentous change
THREE TENS: the need for resolution, difficulties with contracts
TWO TENS: a new direction

THE NINES
FOUR NINES: recognition, a good friend
THREE NINES: success, good health
TWO NINES: administration, handling contracts

THE EIGHTS
FOUR EIGHTS: travel, a lifestyle reversal
THREE EIGHTS: marriage
TWO EIGHTS: new knowledge

THE SEVENS
FOUR SEVENS: intrigue
THREE SEVENS: infirmity
TWO SEVENS: news

THE SIXES
FOUR SIXES: abundance, advantages
THREE SIXES: success, a good social life
TWO SIXES: irritability

THE FIVES
FOUR FIVES: imbalance, discord
THREE FIVES: determination in adversity
TWO FIVES: delay, awaiting a result

THE FOURS
FOUR FOURS: stability, satisfaction
THREE FOURS: reflection, hard work
TWO FOURS: insomnia

THE THREES
FOUR THREES: progress, willpower
THREE THREES: unity
TWO THREES: calm

THE TWOS
FOUR TWOS: handling tension, gathering information
THREE TWOS: indecisiveness
TWO TWOS: accord, balance

THE ACES
FOUR ACES: favorable opportunities, new beginnings
THREE ACES: a small triumph, good news
TWO ACES: partnerships

THE ACES

THE ACES of the minor arcana reveal new themes in life. They can be seen as the primal essences of their suits, denoting action, beginnings, and opportunities. It is helpful to consider the meaning of the suits in terms of their associated elements (see page 21). For example, the suit of Swords is associated with the element of Air—so mental activity, action, and conflict are its values. The Ace of Swords, being the root of the suit, reveals intellectual victory and challenge.

For all the Aces, it is important to make the most of what is on offer, rather than assume that the appearance of these cards will automatically bring you their benefits. They can be seen as gifts—in the Rider Waite deck, each suit icon is handed to the reader from a cloud. As the gift of the Aces is offered to you, so you need to receive its energy, and take action to maximize its potential.

Ace of Cups

Upright Meaning
The suit of Cups is associated with the element of Water, the symbol of flowing emotions. The Ace ushers in a period when emotions and relationships are foremost, and can reveal pregnancy and motherhood. It signifies a phase in which feelings are expressed and reciprocated, and can predict one important love partnership. This is also an auspicious card for creative activities, when original projects get started and inspiration comes naturally.

Reversed Meaning
When reversed, the Ace shows emotions suppressed or out of control, so unhappiness or fears about a relationship may cause concern. There may be worries about children and family, and a lack of understanding between parents or siblings. This is a common card for those struggling to balance home and work. Bear in mind that the Ace in this position often reflects insecurity or fear about the future, not reality. Just as the cup can suddenly overturn, so it can right itself. Sharing your fears is the way forward.

Ace of Pentacles

Upright Meaning
The Ace of Pentacles brings the energy of money, heralding a new era of prosperity. The suit of Pentacles is associated with Earth and, in keeping with this element, the Ace predicts that you will be feeling grounded and realistic. Clever investments, savings schemes, and even spontaneous gambles pay off, and work and business matters are favored. Rather than doubt its authenticity, it is time to appreciate this deserved good fortune.

Reversed Meaning
Imbalance in financial affairs. The Ace reversed can reveal an obsession with money that masks a lack, or neglect, of other responsibilities, so that your priorities are skewed. This is a fruitless pursuit; pinning all your hopes on one outcome alone diverts you from finding the real treasures—the genuine creative projects and people who can bring you emotional comfort. This card may reveal the influences of greed around you, so beware of an acquisitive streak.

Ace of Wands

Upright Meaning

The suit of Wands represents negotiation and creativity. The Ace of Wands is pure fiery masculine energy—as shown by the phallic nature of the wand on Rider-Waite cards, which also bears tiny buds, symbolizing the blossoming of new ventures. This Ace card is a good omen for travel, beginning a new career, or starting a family. It is now time to use your ability to communicate with others to great effectiveness.

Reversed Meaning

In the reversed position, the Ace of Wands can indicate problems with masculinity and creativity—in a woman's reading, it can foretell a relationship in which a male partner lacks commitment, or in which the woman must wait for him. In general, the Ace reversed reveals a degree of separation or delay that blocks results. Partnerships, business dealings, or travel plans may therefore suffer from a lack of organization or poor timing.

Ace of Swords

Upright Meaning

The suit of Swords relates to the element of Air, which is associated with the realm of the intellect. When this card appears in a reading, it shows that your mental agility will bring you success. The Ace also predicts a time of challenge and possible conflict that forces you into action. As this is an innovative card, it foretells mindful energy that will fuel new projects and help you deal assertively with others.

Reversed Meaning

In the reversed position, the Ace of Swords reveals that you are being held back in some way, which leads to frustration and delay. It can indicate a failure of will or lack of confidence in your intellectual abilities. In this instance, the sword is the sword of Damocles, and you are playing an excruciating waiting game. As all Sword cards call upon your innermost resources, believe that you have the strength of character to withstand the situation.

The Twos

Twos stand for balance, partnerships, and the flow of energy between opposites or compatible forces. The Two cards can show the resolution of a problem, the choosing of one course of action over another, depending on their particular suit. With Wands, for example, the suit of negotiation and creativity, the Two reveals a successful dialog that allows you to progress a project; with the martial Swords, the Two suggests a truce when you take a break from a battle of wills. To interpret these cards, look to the partnerships that surround you in the broadest sense, not just your lover. The duos on these cards can reveal anyone with whom you share responsibility, from a babysitter to a business investor.

Two of Cups

Upright Meaning
The upright Two predicts natural harmony between two people. It reveals happy agreements and love, so a relationship may be sealed by an engagement or marriage. Two also sees friendships flourish as you instinctively know how to support and laugh with those around you. Creative partnerships are the message here too, so appreciate those significant others. A writing partner, a fellow musician, or someone with whom you are studying brings you pleasure and inspiration.

Reversed Meaning
As the upright Two shows good communication, so the Two reversed indicates secrets and possibly betrayal. If you are considering a commitment to a partner, it is better to delay your decision until you can really talk with one another. This is a testing time for all relationships when you may not feel you can trust those you usually rely upon. It is best to keep your doubts to yourself just now, and trust only your own judgment.

Two of Pentacles

Upright Meaning
This card reveals business at work—money comes in and goes out and the world turns. This Two predicts financial solvency and productive business partnerships, and there is a trust and fairness in all your dealings. In domestic terms, this card indicates that you will make enough money to run your home as you want it, and achieve some degree of balance between your career and friends and family.

Reversed Meaning
A business partnership suffers when the Two is reversed. Rather than have cooperation, one of you puts in more effort than the other, leading to financial loss. The Two can reveal an unworkable liaison—a colleague or manager may not deliver what they claim. Viewed as an indication of a situation rather than an individual, a new venture may not take off due to lack of funding, which leads to worry and frustration. Take this card as a warning to examine the motives of those whom you choose to trust.

Two of Wands

Upright Meaning

You are moving forward; those who have influence are listening to what you have to say. This card represents great opportunities to put plans into action, to manage your life at all levels, and enjoy the stability that this brings you. The Two heralds faith and partnerships that bring reward, particularly in terms of expanding an existing business or taking a step up in your career. You will receive support and interest from others to ensure steady progress.

Reversed Meaning

In the reversed position, the Two can warn you that your talent may be wasted while others look on. If you value what you do, look elsewhere for likeminded individuals who appreciate your ingenuity. The Two reversed can predict misplaced trust in an unreliable partner: your lover, a friend, a business associate. This, as in all the reversed Twos, is the imbalance to watch out for. Measure your success objectively, and expect others to meet you halfway.

Two of Swords

Upright Meaning

The Two of Swords can be taken literally, as someone you cross swords with in potential conflict. However, it is also a resting position before and after a battle of wits, and, in this sense, the Two reveals a truce or a stalemate. While this may appear to be a welcome respite, you will need to face your opponent eventually. When this thinking time expires, draw on your courage, rely on your intellect, and you will succeed.

Reversed Meaning

The Two reversed reveals a deception, often concerning a partnership. The stalemate of the upright card goes deeper here, as an opponent uses his or her time to manipulate the truth. When this card appears in a reading, it is best not to accept someone else's findings; thoroughly investigate a situation for yourself and be prepared for the defensiveness that liars excel at. It is worth fighting through a web of misdirection to get to the heart of an important matter.

THE MINOR ARCANA

The Threes

One, two, three: go. Three is the point at which everything begins, from blowing out candles on a cake to running a race. Three is the number of creation and life (see page 36), the dynamic synthesis of primal one and balanced two.

As with the other numbers, their suits define just how the Threes are expressed. In the creative suit of Wands, the Three sees the development of an idea into reality; the feudal Three of Swords, however, foretells heartbreak. Unlike the other suit icons, Swords in action maim, whereas Wands together grow.

Three of Cups

Upright Meaning

This is a card of great happiness and a renewed belief in love. Your relationships and those of the people around you develop, so the atmosphere is joyful. Given the harmony of this card, it also brings healing and recovery to those who have felt at a low ebb. It reveals new energy and life, and can also foretell a new baby—literally, or in the form of a precious project. Your social life benefits because there are partnership and christening celebrations, parties, and just the sheer pleasure of feeling close to loved ones.

Reversed Meaning

This Three brings distance and discord. Actual infidelity or an emotional betrayal, no matter how subtle, creates a barrier in partnerships. The potential revealed in the upright card is wasted, so there may be disappointment and disbelief. The Three can also reveal irritating health problems, which in turn are often the result of dissatisfaction and discomfort in emotional matters. Know that this is a false start; you can begin again.

Three of Pentacles

Upright Meaning

You can now do what you do best. The Three of Pentacles is the symbol of the craftsperson, who begins with one idea and from it produces something of value. This is a time of tangible success, when hard work and application bring reward in terms of finances, but also creative satisfaction. You can feel pleased with your achievement because it is the result of your personal effort and vision.

Reversed Meaning

There is an element of a project—or life in general—that you cannot face just now: work itself. You want to have the fruits of your labor without the labor, and perhaps you prefer the ideal to the reality. Consider that poor planning or rushing to complete the least interesting aspects of a job may be at the root of your lethargy. Begin again and get committed to the boring detail as a way to get what you want, or abandon this avenue rather than crave continual distraction.

Three of Wands

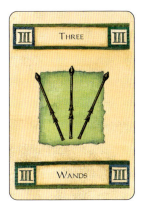

Upright Meaning

This is a time of personal gain and reward when you let others see what motivates you through your work. The Three presents an inspired opportunity for self-expression through art, music, dance, and crafts. Through this, you can assert your individuality, so nurture your quirks and love your eccentricities. Do not be afraid that you will attract negative comments from others; this is an imaginary barrier, and you only have to gain confidence in yourself.

Reversed Meaning

The Three reversed tells of a breakdown in communication. This card shows an inability to express your ideas; inarticulacy makes it impossible for others to visualize or appreciate them. This situation creates tension around you as it is hard to garner support, and you may feel personally anxious because you have no immediate outlet for your creative energies. In this situation, it may be best to slow your pace—declutter your thinking and simplify your plans until this influence shifts.

Three of Swords

Upright Meaning

The Three of Swords reveals loss and heartbreak. In the Rider Waite deck, this is depicted with three swords piercing a heart: a dramatic visualization of how it can feel to be let down by a partner or a dream you held close to your heart. The one solace is that the meaning of the Three is not ambiguous, so when it falls in a future position in a reading it can at least act as a warning. Confront a person or a problem directly; this may cause you pain now, but it is the only way to get to the happier relationships that await.

Reversed Meaning

In the reversed position, heartbreak is accompanied by quarreling and general disorder. Although this sounds more negative, expressing the upheaval can at least release and relieve the tension. This is a tumultuous time, and may be felt as an inner conflict and anxiety rather than pure domestic chaos. Bear in mind that this is a minor arcana card, and its influence is always transient.

The Fours

Fours are even and stable. Four is the number of sides of a square, an ancient symbol for Earth in India and China. In Pythagorean theory, four was the first number to create a solid—the tetrahedron, or pyramid, with a base and three sides. Four relates to structure: the four-armed cross, the four principal compass points, the four elements, and to the organization of the Tarot itself. There are four suits in the deck and four Court cards per suit, leaving forty numbered or "pip" cards.

In a reading, the Fours reveal practical situations rather than esoteric matters. They indicate stability or rigidity, depending again on the qualities of the particular suit. In the emotional suit of Cups, they reveal inaction or boredom, whereas in the suit of Swords, the lack of activity represents a welcome rest from conflict.

Four of Cups

Upright Meaning

The Four of Cups shows an established relationship that feels stuck. This may be temporary, but for the partnership to grow you need to revaluate what brought you together and go forward. Energy and a sense of a shared future are lacking; one or both of you may be feeling restless or mildly bored. In practical terms, nothing is seriously amiss as you continue from day to day, but it is important to express your finer feelings toward each other.

Reversed Meaning

In the reversed position, the Four indicates instability and deadlock; this may result in nervous exhaustion that drains your energy and leaves you feeling low. Equally, this influence could see you submerge yourself in work or other time-hungry tactics to avoid confronting a suffocating situation or relationship. The action you need to take to resolve matters may seem daunting, but you must extricate yourself now to regain your equilibrium.

Four of Pentacles

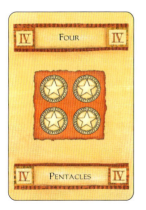

Upright Meaning

Financial security is the message of the upright Four. You may have suffered hardship and have had to work too hard and for too long, but now an enterprise pays out. This is not a great monetary gain, but a period of satisfaction and personal reward. You find relief and can ease off a little, mindful that you have everything you need to keep moving forward. As the pressure eases and you relax, health matters also improve.

Reversed Meaning

The Four reversed shows struggle. This may be because you cannot believe that money may come easily to you and that you are deserving of it. This lack of confidence may not give others the right signals about your talents, and consequently opportunities are missed. This card can also reveal challenging departmental structures at work, internal politics, or simply bad management that marginalizes you and your obvious abilities.

Four of Wands

Upright Meaning

This card is for a great social life and self-establishment. As the suit of Wands buds with ideas, so the tree puts down roots; you may move to a larger home or extend your existing dwelling. Workwise, others show their appreciation of your originality. You are part of every conversation and feel wanted and involved. You can now grow in every aspect of your life, and enjoy it to the full.

Reversed Meaning

The Four reversed reveals the restrictive meaning of the Fours: narrow attitudes block your route to success and may make you feel invisible. As others actively progress and are praised, you feel you don't fit in; this could be your inflexibility, or it could be that the organization or community is conventional and unaccommodating. Whatever the case, examine your motives and those of others carefully, then decide what or who needs to change.

Four of Swords

Upright Meaning

The Four is one of the most positive cards of a difficult suit, because it introduces a time of rest and recuperation after a barrage of stress. This may be physical illness from which you can now fully heal and recover, or a situation where you have had to struggle endlessly just to stay in the game. Whichever applies, it is likely that your strength and energy levels are low, so it is vital that you feel secure from the onslaught and get yourself better.

Reversed Meaning

Whereas the upright Four is a welcome rest, the reversed Four imposes time out. This creates a sense of isolation and possibly resentment that blurs the benefits you may get from being away from home or work. It is better to surrender than fight another's decision, no matter how incomprehensible it may seem. Choose peace; you may feel overruled, but it's not forever.

The Fives

Five is the number of mankind. The five-pointed star is the template for the form of an outstretched human being, with the head, hands, and feet marking each segment. The star is also the emblem of the Hindu god Shiva, who both creates and destroys. This is the double aspect of five: the problems we encounter are manmade—we suffer for them, but can easily extricate ourselves. As we have five fingers, so we have a hand in our own destiny and design.

Unusually, Fives have a similar meaning in all the minor arcana suits. A Five reveals a test: in the suit of Cups this is a test of emotional strength; in Wands, of capability; in Pentacles, of resources; and in Swords, a test of true purpose.

Five of Cups

Upright Meaning
The Five of Cups is the natural outcome of the restless Four. Because small problems in a relationship have been neglected in the past, deeper doubt has taken root. Feelings are no longer hidden and emotions run wild: disappointment, sadness, and regret. This card can often indicate a relationship breaking up, or at least a time of separation when you both take time out to revaluate your partnership. There is, however, an element of relief here; you can stop reacting.

Reversed Meaning
The Five of Cups is one of the few minor arcana cards that has a more positive meaning when reversed. This card reveals that you have reached the lowest point in a particular cycle; you have suffered, but are now further on in the healing process. After suffering rejection on a grand scale, you know that what remains is more hopeful. You see a glimmer of the future before you, and you are now stronger and ready to move on.

Five of Pentacles

Upright Meaning
The obvious meaning of this Five is being poor and feeling lost. It denotes financial difficulties, debt, and its associated stress, but bear in mind that the Five often mirrors a fear of losing money or love, rather than actual scarcity. When this card appears, it indicates that you are feeling cast out and marginalized because having money often means earning a place in society. Martyrdom, whether real or imagined, can be avoided: action rather than passivity will change your circumstances.

Reversed Meaning
A poor decision leaves you feeling impoverished. This is a warning not to cling to possessions or money for their own sake, because what you want may desert you. This applies both to finances and to relationships, so equally you may be on the receiving end of a partner's selfishness, which ultimately endangers your partnership. It is vital to reconsider your priorities now, as your values are under strict scrutiny.

Five of Wands

Upright Meaning

The Five of Wands shows constant challenges to your position. The message here is to remain steadfast rather than instill calm and appease others. Regardless of how well you usually handle pressure, your reputation alone will not rescue you; the conflicts you now face are quite different to those of the past. Rather than go into blithe denial, attend to every detail—double-check travel plans, schedules, accounts, agendas, and appointments.

Reversed Meaning

This Five carries the message of deception. You are hemmed in by another's dishonesty and there is little you can do to change the course of events, other than be clear that you are not to blame. A project may have been well received, then turned down inexplicably in favor of another. As the Wands suit is concerned with negotiation and talking, it is likely that you will have heard words that lead you to conclude you have been dealing with an untruthful or unreliable source. When you know this, let it pass.

Five of Swords

Upright Meaning

What exactly are you fighting for? The battle has been going on for so long that you barely know why it began, or the benefits you thought winning would bring. This is simply a purposeless challenge that can only further deplete your resources. It may be difficult to abandon the cause, but the Five of Swords indicates that you can still walk away with your self-respect. After all, you may simply have overcommitted yourself to hard work without reward.

Reversed Meaning

When the Five is in the upright position, the purpose for battle is thought to be sincere but is found to be meaningless; in the reversed position, the conflict itself is not genuine—purely a show of strength or ego to cover up frailty or incompetence. This may be experienced as others' enjoyment of someone's failure because it makes them feel safer. Endure a moment's embarrassment, admit defeat, and move on.

The Sixes

After the tumultuous Fives, the Sixes denote harmony and passivity. Six forms the Star of David, which comprises one upright and one inverted triangle to represent the soul on Earth—an idea balanced by its expression. The Sixes often reveal two themes or ideas that work together productively, but there is also a sense of hesitation as we see the void between what we have and what is possible. In the book of Genesis, the world was created from chaos in six days, so there is a sense of evolution and history about Six.

Sixes and Fours can be difficult for new readers to differentiate, because they both appear inactive and stable. Imagine that Four signifies order and structure, whereas Six equals contentment and balance. As with all minor arcana cards, the nature of each suit modifies the fundamental meaning of the number. In the suit of Cups, Six reveals the effect of memories on the present; in the creative Six of Wands, the potential for achievement exists, but a confidence gap needs to be bridged.

SIX OF CUPS

UPRIGHT MEANING

When the Six of Cups appears, memories resurface and you reminisce. Mentally, this may be a time when you flit in and out of two worlds: your nostalgic past and happy present. You may meet an old acquaintance who links you with a future project or relationship. In general, this is a time for acknowledging your personal history, appreciating what experience has taught you, and enjoying a new lease of life.

REVERSED MEANING

When the Six of Cups is reversed, a touch of nostalgia becomes sentimentality and a refusal to move on from the past. Inherent in this reverie is the idea that the past is a refuge, a convenient way to avoid present issues that are unsatisfactory. This may be expressed as clinginess toward others, or absorption in their needs to the exclusion of yours. The root of this behavior is the fear of the risks and natural challenges that the present and future hold.

SIX OF PENTACLES

UPRIGHT MEANING

The upright Six of Pentacles shows that there is a beneficent understanding between you and those people who are close to you. During this happy phase you attract genuine help from above— for example, you may receive investment funding for a business from a mentor, a small cash sum, or an unexpected gift from a good friend. These boons, both great and small, show others' appreciation of you and their unstinting support. In return, you give unreservedly to them.

REVERSED MEANING

As the upright Six reveals support and abundance, so the reversed card indicates meanness of spirit and financial withdrawal. Money promised to you will not be forthcoming, or what you are offered is not honestly given or truly available. It is advisable not to accept what little is on offer; hold out for the full amount, or write off the debt rather than buy into a deal or situation that compromises your values.

Six of Wands

Upright Meaning

The upright Six of Wands brings deserved rewards. This can manifest as the favorable resolution of a legal matter, or, at work, you may win a promotion or new contract. There is a sense of triumph here, because now all your hard effort in the past feels truly worthwhile. However, in this card there is also a note of caution: it is a good idea to examine carefully any offers in hand to ensure that all promises made will be fulfilled.

Reversed Meaning

The Six of Wands reversed foretells delays to plans and a fear about their outcome. However, this does not mean you suffer from outright failure—simply a truly frustrating wait, during which you try to discover the right outlet for your dreams. This card can also show that other people may have let you down recently; you may worry about what they are saying behind your back. This atmosphere of insecurity may cause you to feel hesitant.

Six of Swords

Upright Meaning

The upright Six indicates a break from routine and an opportunity to travel, possibly on business or a research trip. This gives you a chance to breathe again and refuel your energy; it may even lead to a valuable discovery of some kind. Do not worry that this time represents closure or an ending — it is just a part of life's natural ebb and flow, during which you can sharpen your wits and return with energy and enthusiasm.

Reversed Meaning

The Six of Swords reversed can reveal a stubborn refusal to see an opportunity. As a result, the world shrinks rather than expands and you feel in limbo. This card can also warn that you cannot rest just now; travel—the gift of this card in the upright position—is not the solution. Unfortunately, you must soldier on rather than escape from trouble. With relentless effort you can work through every problem in turn and gradually go forward.

The Sevens

Seven has a reputation as a mystical number. It was sacred to the god Apollo, founder of the famous Delphic oracle; in classical wisdom it was believed that there were seven planets in the solar system: the Sun, the Moon, Mercury, Venus, Mars, Jupiter, and Saturn; and in Eastern healing there are seven *chakras*, or energy vortexes, in the human body. In folklore, the seventh son of a seventh son was thought to be blessed with magical healing ability.

The most obvious association with seven is the seven days of the week. However, although the seventh day was the day when God rested, rest is not the message of the Tarot Sevens. Number theorists purport that because it is a prime number, indivisible by any other, Seven represents unification. In the Tarot minor arcana, this reveals the bringing together of one's resources. It also represents potential because it is made up of three (the number for heaven) and four (for Earth), indicating the possibility of greatness through integration. In a reading, consider that all the Sevens share this theme of potential and the need for integrity and perception.

Seven of Cups

Upright Meaning

The Seven of Cups reveals that you may question a recent offer. You are following a dream, but make sure that this opportunity will deliver. Confusion and indecision abound with this card, so you have only your instinct to rely upon. To banish doubt, retrace your reactions and remember your first impression, rather than the reasoned arguments that may have followed. This is a time of great creativity; just ensure that whatever or whomever you are now dealing with is worthy of you.

Reversed Meaning

The reversed Seven indicates the danger of idealizing a person or potential event in order to avoid an unpalatable truth. You may be so keen to succeed, or your desires so overwhelming, that you delude yourself. An alternative meaning of this card is that you are deceived not by your own fantasies but by a lover. The message is not to take anything for granted.

Seven of Pentacles

Upright Meaning

The Seven of Pentacles tells you that you must keep on going, because there is more on offer. Work on a long-term project looks promising, but it is not time to rest yet—plans for your home or business will come to fruition, but only with steady application and willpower. Believe that your goal is worthwhile, and visualize what you want by achieving it. This card often applies to tedious jobs, in both your career and home, and its message is unrelenting, too: persevere.

Reversed Meaning

Like the upright Seven of Pentacles, the reversed card also reveals the need to act. However, this is because progress in non-existent: time has been wasted, and money problems may be the result of doing too little too late—or nothing at all. Opportunities will dwindle and anxiety about finances will only fester, so surrender to your conscience or risk a greater loss.

Seven of Wands

Upright Meaning
Just as the Seven of Pentacles urges action, so the Seven of Wands shows the need to keep talking in spite of all the difficult debate or arguments around you. Think that you have six physical wands to your side, and that the seventh lies in your path; this seventh wand is your only obstacle, which can be overcome by confidence and past experience. Look at this barrier up close; it is only one more piece of debris, which will disappear if you stay true to your purpose.

Reversed Meaning
In the reversed position, the Seven shows serious concerns about the work you are doing. A project or current contract may feel unworkable and without purpose, which in turn causes you to doubt your position. At this time, there are simply too many challenging issues to deflect or resolve. It is best to conserve your energy and do whatever is necessary to allay stress; put yourself first.

Seven of Swords

Upright Meaning
As the Sevens indicate the need for perception, the martial Seven of Swords calls for an expert battle strategy and razor-sharp wit to disarm an adversary. You may be feeling cornered and pursued by a difficult opponent, but your creative intellect may prove to be your best ally. When trapped, you may even resort to deviousness: do whatever is reasonably necessary to extricate yourself from the situation. Rely on your mental agility to sift the truth from the lies.

Reversed Meaning
The Seven of Swords reversed can reveal that you give up on a fight too soon. Be adamant about what you want, and be prepared to make a forceful stand for it rather than give in to others' manipulation. Protect your interests on a practical level, too: double-check home security and keep valuables close. Otherwise, you may fall prey to the dishonest.

THE EIGHTS

THE EIGHTS IN THE minor arcana signify change. This may appear inconsistent with the other even numbers—two, four, and six—which indicate stability, as the natural tension of opposites is balanced. However, as the numbered minor arcana suits run from the Aces (the gifts of the suits) to the completion of the Tens, the Eights hold the history of our experience. With this knowledge, life-changing decisions can be taken.

Eight is associated with the Greek god Hermes because the number forms the shape of the magic wand, or caduceus, that he carried. It is also the lemniscate that appears on the Magician and Strength cards (see pages 68 and 88). Hermes was the gods' messenger, and he and his number are associated with movement and change. Although change can bring anxiety, its purpose is renewal. Baptismal fonts have eight sides as a symbol of regeneration.

In the Eights, there is also the need for assessment and judgment based on self-acceptance. The Eight of Cups, for example, denotes a considered change of heart. The Eight of Wands reveals an adjustment to a faster pace of life, but also a time to reap reward.

Eight of Cups

Upright Meaning

The Eight of Cups reveals dissatisfaction with a particular relationship, or more generally with the way in which you are relating to other people. There may be no fault with the other party, but you turn away in order to seek what you need elsewhere. This is a difficult decision that you must take to protect yourself in the long term, rather than live from day to day in the knowledge that something is not quite right.

Reversed Meaning

As you might expect, the reversed Eight of Swords shows an error of judgment. You may walk away from a great established relationship or other important partnership opportunity because you cannot appreciate its worth. Whereas the upright Eight of Swords reveals a mature decision, here immaturity prevails. Alternatively, you may be the victim of another's poor judgment when they abandon you in order to satisfy their ego elsewhere.

Eight of Pentacles

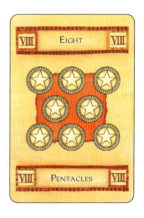

Upright Meaning

The Eight reveals money on its way to you. This brings a sense of liberation and the belief that doing what you love can support you financially. This card is also a sign that educational study will lead to a profession and a satisfying career or project. What you focus on now will be the bedrock of your material security and self-esteem. You can truly value yourself and feel valued by others.

Reversed Meaning

A need for money diverts your energies so that your ambition becomes fragmented. You may lose the bigger picture and find it hard to see your way through a deluge of essential tasks that only dilute your perspective. In practice, the Eight reversed can show that you are motivated solely by money, possibly because a soul-destroying project or job has little else to offer you. Don't neglect your need for a pay check, but appreciate what you have to offer—and take that talent elsewhere.

Eight of Wands

Upright Meaning

The Eight of Wands is perhaps the most positive of the Eights, for it heralds wonderful news. This is a fast and frantic time when offers come to you naturally. You may have an opportunity to travel; to partake in a creative collaboration; be inspired by talking to stimulating individuals; or find a way to contribute to a community project. Rise to the challenge and believe that you can have it all. This is a time for you to shine.

Reversed Meaning

In the reversed position, the Eight of Wands shows a degree of confusion because you cannot seem to connect with those you want to deal with, or assess what it is that they are offering you. When you try to communicate with others, you miss the mark: letters go astray, or phone messages and emails disappear. Talking or writing to them will not clarify issues; all you can do is be patient. Avoid making important journeys or signing agreements just now.

Eight of Swords

Upright Meaning

There is an element of embarrassment at work when the Eight of Swords appears. For example, a project goes wrong, or a deal falls through unexpectedly; whatever your circumstances, this turn of fortune could feel catastrophic. However, rather than admit it immediately, you shield yourself with pride, although inside you panic. At this time, it is vital to admit defeat and ask for help, rather than let failure fester.

Reversed Meaning

The Eight of Swords reversed reveals frustration, and in some cases outright despair and anger. You may feel furious with yourself and lash out at others because you need an outlet for your inability to accept a difficult situation. The way out is to drop your defences a little; you may suffer a moment's humiliation by telling the truth, but this could free you from a punitive deadlock. A solution awaits: use your head, rather than lose it.

The Nines

Nines are known as the "ultimates" of their suits, where the intrinsic value of each suit finds maximum expression. Nine represents the triple triad of mind, body, and spirit; it also expresses order. There are nine choirs of angels, and, in Taoism, nine numbered squares complete the Lo Shu, the magical template that is used to calculate the effects of time and *chi* energy on a building. In this sense, the Nines express the idea of foundation.

With the Nines, it is helpful to recall the suit meanings and then mentally develop them to their utmost. As Cups represent the emotions, the Nine crowns you with happiness; Wands, for creativity and communication, reveal great satisfaction and dialog; and Earth-bound Pentacles reveal a great material gain. As ever, the troublesome Swords represent ultimate conflict. However, as with all battles, there is always an outcome and a way to move forward.

Nine of Cups

Upright Meaning

The Nine of Cups is often referred to as the "wish card" in a reading. It means that a dream may come true; everything you hope for can become reality. This abundant card shows a surfeit of affection and fun, and a perfect balance in all your relationships. This is a time for wonderful social opportunities, new friendships, and intimate partnerships. There is a natural flow about life now, and health matters are also favored.

Reversed Meaning

In the reversed position, the Nine shows imbalance in the realm of the affections. This may manifest as self-absorption, when you neglect those closest to you, alienating friends and lovers in the process. Alternatively, you may feel sidelined by another person's obsession with me, me, me—which could see you clinging to them all the more. As the upright card shows an easy connection with others, so the Nine reversed reveals delays or emotional disconnection.

Nine of Pentacles

Upright Meaning

The Nine of Pentacles shows a time for spoiling yourself. You have achieved great material stability through hard work and financial acumen, and now you have time for leisure. For the organized, you can enjoy putting your house in order or tending the garden, and generally prizing your status. Small problems are resolved and domestic peace abounds. Your natural contentment is attractive to others, so be prepared for a meeting of minds.

Reversed Meaning

Your domestic sanctuary may be under siege when the Nine of Pentacles reverses. Irresponsibility with money, or an unwillingness to deal with debts or confront disputes, leaves you vulnerable to feelings of insecurity. To safeguard your home and heal the predicament, you need to take a more reasonable approach to problem-solving. Look at alternatives, rather than stubbornly holding out at any cost. When you do this, a resolution is possible.

Nine of Wands

Upright Meaning

You are, and need to be, at your most ingenious when the Nine of Wands appears. Expend your energy cleverly to make the work you do go further—schedule your tasks (from business meetings to shopping) and plan your social activities carefully. You are amazingly strong now and have the support of others around you, including financial help, should you need it. With consideration, you can enjoy this creative but demanding time.

Reversed Meaning

The Nine of Wands reversed reveals that you may be drowning under others' constant demands on your time, which are draining you. There is little satisfaction to be gained when you can only be concerned with completion rather than enjoying the journey. It is best not to give in to other people's pressure on any account, although unfortunately this can become a way of life. Distance yourself and spend more time on considering your own needs, rather than appeasing people who give you so little just now.

Nine of Swords

Upright Meaning

As is so typical of the suit of Swords, the ultimate nature of the Nine implies suffering, due to others' unfair dealings or because illness has sapped all your energy. In this situation it is almost natural to feel like a victim and give in. However, the best course of action is to rely on your astuteness, be patient with yourself, and you will regain your equilibrium. Consider that the stress you may be suffering from begins in the mind, not the body, so start by bolstering your confidence.

Reversed meaning

Unfortunately, the reversed Nine of Swords shows a maximizing of the unhappiness of the upright card. In this instance there is a real sense of despair and entrapment. However, you can get through this testing time if you can adjust your view of your situation. Ask for help from everyone and you will find a way to resurrect your faith in the future.

The Tens

Tens stand for completeness and perfection. Ten is also a mystic number with myriad examples of its importance—the Ten Commandments of the Old Testament; the astrological decan, or ten degrees of a zodiac sign, as a predictor of personality types; the ten spheres, or aspects of God, on the Tree of Life in Hebrew mysticism. As the Nines re-establish the ultimate values of each suit, so the Tens present them in their fullness. When the cycle is complete, it begins again, so the idea of Ten encompasses endings and beginnings; one plus zero equals one. Just as countdowns begin with Ten, in the same way the end of a decade is anticipated as a turning point, a new era.

In the minor arcana suits, the Ten's sheer number can reveal the greatest happiness or the heaviest burdens. The Ten of Wands reveals the weight of the world on your shoulders; in Cups, the love of family and its generations is predicted; in the suit of Swords, the focus moves from the individual in conflict to groups; and in Pentacles, the Ten represents the most that money can bring.

Ten of Cups

Upright Meaning

The Ten of Cups reveals complete contentment in all relationships. It highlights the love of a family for one another, and this encompasses family in its broadest sense—from lovers and children to close networks of friends and business partnerships. The Ten brings a sense of perfect togetherness and achievement, and an appreciation of your place at home and in the wider world. This is a time of perfect peace and harmony.

Reversed Meaning

The Ten reversed expresses the loosening of family ties and disruption to your social circle. Close friends move away—physically or emotionally—due to a development in their own lives which may leave a gap in yours. Consider that this card can arise if you are afraid of losing someone, and when there is a feeling of unrest due to something being taken from a family or group. This can manifest as a newcomer who brings an unwelcome influence. The upside is that the situation is temporary; normality will return.

Ten of Pentacles

Upright Meaning

The Ten of Pentacles in the upright position reveals inheritance, generosity, and possibly a love match that brings a wealth of love and happiness. The flavor of this card is also maturity, in terms of maturing investment policies, and also emotional wisdom. This is a time to enjoy the abundance of a family, and benefit from the shared resources and values that flow from one generation to the next.

Reversed Meaning

Inevitably, the Ten reversed shows adversity concerning family money and property, and can reveal a love mismatch that is based on status rather than emotional bonds. There is a rigidity implied here too, where the expectations of older generations clash with those of younger members. The outcome is disconnection rather than dialog; values are not shared and money issues become contentious.

Ten of Wands

Upright Meaning

If the Ten of Wands is the first card to appear in a reading, you may want to reshuffle the deck and lay the cards again; the Ten is often a signal that you are overburdened and need to take more time in order to be receptive to the reading. The meaning of the Ten is that you are carrying the weight of the world, with all its attendant pressures. It is better to discard a little responsibility by choice, rather than drop all ten Wands because you cannot continue. The Ten may also indicate a burden of guilt.

Reversed Meaning

The Ten of Wands reversed is a message that you need to lighten up, for the burdens that you carry are more imagined than actual. You may believe that others' demands on you are the sole cause of your predicament, but it may be easier to blame them than destroy the illusion of your own importance. When you stop diverting your energies to the needs of others, you will be able to care for yourself more effectively.

Ten of Swords

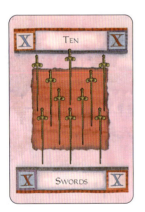

Upright Meaning

The Ten of Swords often relates to a group of people rather than an individual. It reveals the accumulation of difficulties that finally reach their natural outcome, so an era ends in high drama—and possibly in ruin. In your career, a business may fall; equally a social group may suffer discord to the extent that broken bonds seem irreparable. The comfort of this card is a relief from conflict, and the knowledge that what has happened was unavoidable.

Reversed Meaning

In the reversed position, the meaning of the upright card stands. However, because more strife is unfortunately to come, you may feel besieged by worry. The prospect of failure or conflict, however, is often more angst-ridden that the event itself; all you can focus on now is managing your state of mind to stave off despair. The world will turn, and you with it.

The Pages

The Pages of the minor arcana are usually described as young people or children. However, their interpretation can be much more encompassing: the Pages are Peter Pans, so they include character types (both male and female) who are young at heart—Geminis, for example, have a reputation for this. The quality of youth is also significant, because it shows a young situation, or a new influence in your life. The type of influence is again determined according to the element of each suit—emotional, idealistic, financial, or intellectual. Pages are also messengers, the heralds of budding energies; in this way they can be seen as transformational links, revealing just how you get from one place in life to another. Like the Queens and Kings, they can show aspects of the self.

All the Pages in the minor arcana are associated with the element of Earth, which is modified by their suit element. The Page of Swords, for instance, is Earth of the suit of Air. Earth and Air together indicate practical affairs and mentality, so this Page brings you helpful intelligence that you can put to good use. The reversed Page shows the misuse of information: slander or malicious gossip. However, consider that the Pages do not possess the higher energy of the Knights, Queens, or Kings: they are younger, and can be passed over. As transformational links, their influence soon passes. The dual energies of each card are listed below its title as an aid to interpretation.

Page of Cups
Earth of The Suit of Water

Upright Meaning
The Page of Cups is a sociable, intuitive spirit who just loves good company and the good life. Traditionally, he is seen as artistic: he is the archetypal creative dreamer. He runs his life by his feelings, symbolized by Water, the element of his suit. As a messenger, he has positive news about relationships and children. His presence can be reassuring, particularly if he arrives after a spell of emotional insecurity.

Reversed Meaning
The reversed Page is a young person who is unable to express his feelings in a mature way. He regresses to childishness, from bouts of temper to tears and sulks, in order to get the attention that he craves. His message is fraught and possibly incomplete; you cannot get the whole story from this person, so in a reading, his influence is ultimately one of frustration.

Page of Pentacles
Earth of The Suit of Earth

Upright Meaning
The Page of Pentacles can be described as a hard-working, methodical young person. He is reliable, willing to take responsibility for his actions, and is dedicated to serving others. He brings a message that good news about your financial affairs is to come. His appearance in your reading can also act as advice or a gentle warning: that a diligent attitude will help you to manage any existing or future financial pressures.

Reversed Meaning
The Page reversed can be likened to an errant teenager with a lethal weapon: your credit card. There is a fine line, however, between theft and taking what he thinks he has a natural right to. This card reveals extravagance and irresponsibility. The Page's message here is that you may be restricted, due to someone else taking too much away from you.

THE MINOR ARCANA

PAGE OF WANDS
EARTH OF THE SUIT OF FIRE

UPRIGHT MEANING

The Wands bring conversations and conditions for success, so the Page is an inventive youth who is a natural communicator. As his elements are Earth and Fire, his message is practical and urgent. Yet while his enthusiasm is infectious, the Fire can burn out, leaving you to do the legwork. This card can reveal a brilliant idea that quickly fizzles out, so check out the facts before the Page bewitches you entirely.

REVERSED MEANING

The Page reversed can show a young person who is not communicative, and who may be holding back the truth. When he makes an appearance in a reading, messages are delayed rather than delivered. This card can also reveal deception through charm. His words are empty, and it is unlikely that any promises he makes will be kept. Try to recognize him, and beware his limitations.

PAGE OF SWORDS
EARTH OF THE SUIT OF AIR

UPRIGHT MEANING

The Page of Swords has incisive wit and perception, and brings good intelligence, along with helpful people who take swift action to help your cause. As an individual, this younger person is bright beyond his or her years. The Page's message is that you must rely on your brain to stay ahead; this is a time when your mind begins to earn you success in business or education.

REVERSED MEANING

The reversed Page is secret poison, manipulating people through misinformation and lies. As a go-between he stirs up trouble, and cannot be relied upon to be accurate about any arrangement: he deals purely in hearsay with a twist. His message signifies the beginning of malicious gossip or slander, or being unjustly treated in general. As with all Pages, he does not carry the weight of the higher Court cards; step over him and ignore the meddling.

The Knights

THE KNIGHTS ARE the seekers of the minor arcana. Just as the Pages begin courtly life as messengers and graduate to Knights, so the Knights symbolize stamina and energy. They reveal the speeding up of events. As their qualities are essentially martial, the suits of Pentacles and Swords suit them well. The suits of Cups and Wands, however, can clash a little with the action-driven Knight, whose more emotional or idealistic nature may be in conflict with his apparent commitment to action.

All the Knights in the minor arcana are associated with the element of Air, which is modified by their suit element. The Knight of Swords, for example, is Air of the suit of Air. Double Air indicates action, conflict, and mental agility, so this Knight brings battles, but can also herald a sharp-witted individual who hurtles into your life and departs at speed. The dual energies of each card are listed below its title as an aid to interpretation.

KNIGHT OF CUPS
AIR OF THE SUIT OF WATER

UPRIGHT MEANING

As Knights are action cards, an emotional Knight may not make the ideal combatant. His appearance in a reading reveals a dreamy, affectionate individual who brings with him new friends for you. However, as a potential lover, he may not get around to expressing his feelings, and he can appear somewhat remote. His actions—or lack of them—may leave you feeling confused. What is he offering you?

REVERSED MEANING

The negative traits of the upright Knight of Cups are magnified in the reversed position: this Knight cannot be trusted to keep a promise, turn up for an appointment, or acknowledge your feelings in any way. He may think that he is being bohemian and romantic; it is advisable that you cure him of his fantasy. After all, he could let you down badly.

KNIGHT OF PENTACLES
AIR OF THE SUIT OF EARTH

UPRIGHT MEANING

The Knight of Pentacles comes with a guarantee: travel with him and you get where you need to go. The journey ahead may not be inspiring, however, but this steady, loyal character can be relied upon to make headway in business matters and find practical solutions to problems. Viewed as a situation, the upright Knight of Pentacles reveals that consistent effort will ensure progress in all your financial affairs.

REVERSED MEANING

The Knight reversed pontificates, does little, and is dull. At best he is a ditherer, at worst a thief. When this card appears in a reading, it warns of financial impropriety and complacency. It is therefore best to play detective when dealing with any new financial advisors or institutions; naturally, make sure you check the small print of all policies and other contracts.

Knight of Wands
Air of The Suit of Fire

Upright Meaning
The Knight of Wands is a passionate, liberal character who gets things moving; his irrepressible personality, however, can mean that he needs to indulge his dreams without others' interference. As a situation, this Knight symbolizes a creative time during which decisions are made and, as with the other Knights, events speed up. Some readers say that the appearance of this card reveals a house move.

Reversed Meaning
The Knight of Wands in the reversed position appears to make a contribution to an important project, but he is doing little except reveling in the attention that he gets from his new-found status. This card unfortunately reveals insincerity and apparent action, delay, and ensuing confusion. You may, therefore, need to protect yourself from a dangerous egotist.

Knight of Swords
Air of The Suit of Air

Upright Meaning
Like the King of Swords, as a personality, the Knight can indicate the arrival of a professional, such as a doctor or lawyer. His charisma is disarming, and his challenging personality beguiling; he does, however, overlook the detail. He brings with him necessary battles that must be fought. As a fast mover in a suit famed for action, this Knight represents a great surge of energy: events in your life speed up, and a drama unfolds.

Reversed Meaning
The Knight of Swords reversed is a coward who does not do what he says he does. On the surface, he may appear to be forthright and loquacious; however, he has no courage or true conviction. When interpreting him as a situation rather than a person, this Knight warns that someone whom you rely upon as an ally cannot be trusted to stay the distance.

THE MINOR ARCANA

The Queens

Traditionally, the Queens represent the influences of women as individuals; in a woman's reading, the Queen can represent the self in the significator position (see pages 38, 39, 40, 55, 59). To identify her elsewhere, one astrological technique is to consider the element of a Queen's suit and relate it to one of three possible Sun signs—for example, the Queen of Cups is ruled by Water, so she may reveal a mature woman born under the sign of Scorpio, Cancer, or Pisces. The four Queens of the minor arcana can also be seen as four aspects of major arcana card III, the Empress: emotional and nurturing (Cups); creative (Wands); abundant and practical (Pentacles); and intelligent and protective (Swords).

Many readers have difficulty interpreting the Queen and the other Court cards as real personalities in their lives. One answer is to return to the elemental approach, and consider the Queens as distinct energies rather than people. The Queens then reveal how you deal with a situation, and the forces that motivate you at a given time.

Each Court card can also be assigned an elemental energy, in addition to the element of the suit. The feminine Queens are Water, plus the suit element: so the Queen of Cups is Water of the suit of Water. Double water indicates ultimate femininity— associated in Tarot with intensity of emotion. The dual energies of each card are listed below its title as an aid to interpretation.

THE MYSTERY OF THE TAROT

QUEEN OF CUPS
WATER OF THE SUIT OF WATER

UPRIGHT MEANING

The upright Queen of Cups is the Queen of Hearts: she represents love and natural beauty. She is sociable, sensitive, and artistic, and her emotions rule her world. Faithful and nurturing, the Queen gives unconditionally to those around her. Intuition and perception are also highlighted when she appears, so this is a time to take note of your dreams. Within them, you may find hidden messages that help you follow your heart.

REVERSED MEANING

The Queen of Cups reversed is a competitive socialite who often thrives on other people's attention, yet she gives little in return. Her influence is draining and she is often envious. It is wise to take her seriously, as she is the queen of broken hearts: her appearance masks a deceptive and unreliable nature. In a relationship, she may be jealous and faithless.

QUEEN OF PENTACLES
WATER OF THE SUIT OF EARTH

UPRIGHT MEANING

Generosity is the meaning of the upright Queen of Pentacles. She may appear as a mentor, in business or a family; this successful older woman has wisdom and funds at her disposal and uses them appropriately. She is a multitasker, managing her finances, property, and relationships well, but she also knows when to spend money on herself. She is a source of inspiration and practical support.

REVERSED MEANING

When reversed, this Queen uses money as a weapon with which to control others. She has little emotional literacy, and so expresses her insecurity through her spending patterns. Crashing between miserliness and extravagance, she brings a roller-coaster of instability and cannot be trusted to relate to others in a balanced way. This individual is difficult to negotiate with; observe her actions, but stay distant.

Queen of Wands
Water of The Suit of Fire

Upright Meaning

This Queen has a magic wand with which to do her bidding. Her qualities are creativity, both practical (deriving from the phallic nature of the wand) and cerebral; independence, and loquaciousness. Sociable, forward-looking, and nurturing, the Queen of Wands reveals a woman who is in touch with her intimate needs and long-term ambitions, and who in turn deals sensitively with the needs of others.

Reversed Meaning

The Queen of Wands reversed takes on more than she can handle. She is overprotective, and wants involvement in order to feel included. This, however, feels oppressive for those to whom she is closest. Her motivation may be pure, but what she says she can achieve is never demonstrated. In this way, she is unreliable and cannot keep her word.

Queen of Swords
Water of The Suit of Air

Upright Meaning

This Queen is defined by her mental alacrity. Her company is stimulating and she uses her shining intelligence to entertain, enthrall, and challenge those around her. Forthright and graceful, she relies on logic rather than emotion to run her life. Her strength of character makes her a loyal friend, but in following true reason, she tends to her own needs first before extending help to others.

Reversed Meaning

The Queen reversed turns her sword on others, and may look for excuses to do so. Sharp-tongued to the point of brutality, she knows how to use words as a weapon. These are the actions of a bitter individual who may pose as a moralist. Ironically, she twists the truth and the knife when vengeance calls. Avoid the double edge of her sword at all costs.

THE KINGS

TRADITIONALLY, the Kings represent the influences of a mature man; in a woman's reading, the King can represent her partner; or he may symbolize aspects of the self for both men and women, particularly if he appears in the significator position in a spread (see pages 38, 39, 40, 55, 59). As with the Queens (see page 149), one identification technique is to consider the element of a King's suit and relate it to one of three possible Sun signs—for example, the King of Pentacles is ruled by Earth, so he may indicate a Taurean, Virgoan, or Capricorn man. The Kings of the minor arcana can also be seen as four aspects of card IV, the Emperor, who represents order and rulership. When applying this to the suits, we get the following correspondences: mastery of emotions (Cups); strength and compassion (Wands); financial management (Pentacles); ideas and action (Swords).

Again, as with the Queens, an alternative interpretation can be gleaned by using an elemental approach, viewing the Kings as distinct energies rather than people. In this context, the Kings can show your motivating influences, illuminating how you respond to situations revealed in the surrounding cards.

Each Court card can also be assigned an elemental energy, in addition to the element of the suit. All the masculine Kings are Fire, plus their suit element: so the King of Swords is Fire of the suit of Air. Fire and Air together give the energy and passion of Fire with the studied logic and quick-wittedness of Air, so this King is interpreted as a whirlwind of ideas and action, but without steady purpose—the fire dwindles and he moves on. The dual energies of each card are listed below its title as an aid to interpretation.

King of Cups
Fire of The Suit of Water

Upright Meaning
The King of Cups may be an arts administrator, or at least a lover of the arts. He is kindly, reliable, and highly sociable; he follows his intuition when making decisions. As a master of the emotions, at best he is sensitive to others' feelings; at worst he endeavors to control his own feelings, which makes him seem distant and difficult to pin down. His appearance in a reading can signify your head ruling your heart; it is better to use both faculties.

Reversed Meaning
The King of Cups reversed, unlike the upright King, shows feelings out of control. This can manifest in destructive behavior patterns, such as a refusal to discuss important issues or acting to disrupt a situation rather than manage it. He is emotionally vulnerable, and expresses this in an immature way.

King of Pentacles
Fire of The Suit of Earth

Upright Meaning
The King of Pentacles in the upright position is King Midas. Often a corporate man, he is the business manager or other professional who is adept at his work: he problem-solves, deals, and ultimately accrues wealth. Generous and thoroughly reliable, he brings material comfort and practical support. As a predictive force, he heralds resolutions and reward.

Reversed Meaning
The King of Pentacles reversed can be a dangerous opponent. It is important that he wins at all cost, and therefore is untrustworthy when dealing with any cause other than his own. Integrity and a good reputation are less important to him than immediate gain. This King brings debt and insecurity, particularly pertaining to property matters: he may manifest in your life as the corrupt landlord, builder, or real estate agent whose greed comes first.

King of Wands
Fire of The Suit of Fire

Upright Meaning
The King of Wands is a resilient entrepreneur, a traveler who loves exploration and freedom. As a father figure he is protective, but he also understands his family's needs to express themselves as individuals in their own right. This gives him a maturity and wisdom that naturally attract others to him. He treats those around him with honor: there is no desire to direct and control them in order to gain their respect.

Reversed Meaning
The King reversed has a narrow mindset. As his upright twin comprehends the need for a free spirit, so this negative ruler is a strict disciplinarian. He is the overbearing father or boss, but here tinged with bitterness or bigotry. As an indicator of your feelings, the King can reveal resentment. As you would not rely on him, do not act out the need for vengeance.

King of Swords
Fire of The Suit of Air

Upright Meaning
The King of Swords is a master of the mind; he relies on his wits and his ambition is clear. Willing to fight for the prize, he is comfortable in conflict and will not flinch when challenged. He makes fast judgments, and may be an influential business person or professional, such as a doctor or solicitor. However, because he thrives on strife and adrenalin, he loses interest in the lull between one project and the next.

Reversed Meaning
The King of Swords reversed represents dangerous opposition. He wields his sword ruthlessly and his mental violence is relentless. When he appears in a reading, you may be dealing with someone who will try to outwit you in any way he can, playing a cruel game of cat and mouse. It is best to run rather than risk any contact with him.

APPENDICES

TAROT RESOURCES

BIBLIOGRAPHY

The Art of Tarot, Liz Dean, Cico Books, 2001

Tarot: An Illustrated Guide, Jonathan Dee, D & S Books, 2000

The Tarot, Alfred Douglas, Penguin, 1988

Sasha Fenton's Fortune Telling by Tarot Cards, Sasha Fenton, Zambezi Publishing, 2002

The Complete Illustrated Guide to Tarot, Rachel Pollack, Element Books, 1999

The Pictorial Key to the Tarot, Arthur Edward Waite, Samuel Weiser, Inc., 2000

A History of Playing Cards, Roger Tilley, Studio Vista, 1973

The Tarot: Art, Mysticism, and Divination, Sylvie Simon, Alpine Fine Arts Collection, 1986

The Encyclopedia of Tarot (Vol. I), Stuart R. Kaplan, U.S. Games Systems, Inc., 2001

The Complete Book of Tarot, Juliet Sharman-Burke, Pan Books, 1985

Initiation into the Tarot, Naomi Ozaniec, Watkins Publishing, 2002

WEBSITES

www.tarothermit.com

www.tarotgarden.com

CARDS

The Visconti-Sforza Tarot is a generic term referring to a number of editions of the Tarots painted for the Visconti and Sforza families. These decks are usually dated between 1428 and 1450 and are named after the collections in which they are presently held. The three principal Visconti-Sforza Tarots are the Pierpont Morgan-Bergamo (presented throughout this volume); the Cary Yale, and the Brera. Some Tarot scholars believe that these decks were painted to commemorate important dates in the history of the families, such as the wedding of Filippo Visconti and Maria de Savoy in 1428; the marriage of Bianca-Maria Visconti and Francesco Sforza in 1441; and 1450, when Francesco Sforza was crowned Duke of Milan. There is much debate over which deck commemorated which occasion. For further reading on this, I highly recommend Stuart R. Kaplan's *Encyclopedia of Tarot*, Volume I, as listed in the bibliography above.

To obtain the Visconti Tarot and the other Lo Scarabeo decks reproduced in this volume, contact:

www.loscarabeo.com

To obtain Tarot cards produced by Urania Verlag AG Müller, contact:

www. tarot.com

THE MYSTERY OF THE TAROT

PICTURE CREDITS

Title page: Justice, Visconti Tarots, Lo Scarabeo Edizioni D'Arte.

Page 2: Top left: The Chariot; top right, the Fool; below left; the Emperor; below right: Strength. Visconti Tarots, Lo Scarabeo Edizioni D'Arte.

Page 3: Judgment, Liguria Piedmont Tarot, Lo Scarabeo Edizioni D'Arte.

Page 5: Detail from the Moon, Oswald Wirth Tarot, Bridgeman Art Library.

Page 6 The Sun, Classic Tarot, Lo Scarabeo Edizioni D'Arte.

Page 7 Cloud card from the Dante Tarot, Lo Scarabeo Edizioni D'Arte.

Page 8 Justice, Charles VI (Grigonneur) Tarot, Bridgeman Art Library.

Page 9 Above: The High Priestess, Visconti Tarots, Lo Scarabeo Edizioni D'Arte. Below: The Page of Wands, Guildhall Library, London.

Page 10: The Fool, Tarot of Marseilles, Mary Evans Picture Library.

Page 11: The Crocodile, Grand Tarot Belline, Bridgeman Art Library.

Page 12: The Magician, Visconti Tarots, Lo Scarabeo Edizioni D'Arte.

Page 13: Left: The Knight of Cups, Visconti Tarots, Lo Scarabeo Edizioni D'Arte. Right: The Knight of Swords, Tarot of Marseilles, Mary Evans Picture Library.

Page 14: The Ace of Swords, Ligurian Piedmont Tarot, Lo Scarabeo Edizioni D'Arte.

Page 15: The Ace of Cups, Guildhall Library, London.

Page 16: From The Egyptian Tarot, Lo Scarabeo Edizioni D'Arte.

Page 17: The Moon, The Tarot of the Sphinx, Lo Scarabeo Edizioni D'Arte.

Page 18: The Chariot, Oswald Wirth Tarot, Mary Evans Picture Library.

Page 19: Left: Judgment, copyright 2002 Beth Moon. All rights reserved. Right: The Lovers, Rider Waite Tarot, Bridgeman Art Library.

Page 20: The Ace of Coins, Minchiate Florentine, Lo Scarabeo Edizioni D'Arte.

Page 21: The Emperor, Minchiate Florentine, Lo Scarabeo Edizioni D'Arte.

Page 23: From left to right: The Star, the Sun, and the Moon, Visconti Tarots, Lo Scarabeo Edizioni D'Arte.

Pages 24, 25: The Fool and the Tower, Etteilla Spanish Tarot, Bridgeman Art Library.

Page 26: From the Tree of Life Tarot, Urania Verlag AG Müller.

Page 28: Detail of the Hermit , Oswald Wirth Tarot, Mary Evans Picture Library.

Page 29: Top: Detail of the Moon, Rider Waite Tarot, Bridgeman Art Library. Center: Detail of the Knight of Swords, Tarot of Marseilles, Mary Evans Picture Library. Bottom: Detail of Strength, Visconti Tarots, Lo Scarabeo Edizioni D'Arte.

Page 30: Detail from the Moon, Oswald Wirth Tarot, Bridgeman Art Library.

Page 31: Top: Detail of Temperance. Center right: detail of the Empress. Left: detail of the High Priestess, all from the Visconti Tarots, Lo Scarabeo Edizioni D'Arte.

Page 32: The Queen of Coins, Tarot of Marseilles, Mary Evans Picture Library.

THE MINOR ARCANA

Page 33: Right: The Star, Crystal Tarot, Lo Scarabeo Edizioni D'Arte. Left: The Two of Coins, Zigeuner Tarot, Urania Verlag AG Müller.

Page 34: From The I Ching of Love, Lo Scarabeo Edizioni D'Arte.

Page 60: Left: The Tower; center: the World; right: the Wheel of Fortune, Visconti Tarots, Lo Scarabeo Edizioni D'Arte.

Pages 66, 68, 70, 72, 74, 76, 78, 80, 82, 84, 86, 88, 90, 92, 94, 96, 98, 100, 102, 104, 106, 108: Major arcana from The Visconti Tarots, Lo Scarabeo Edizioni D'Arte.

Page 111: The Ace of Cups, Tarot of Marseilles, Mary Evans Picture Library.

Page 113: The Ace of Cups, Visconti Tarots, Lo Scarabeo Edizioni D'Arte.

Page 116: The Two of Swords, Visconti Tarots, Lo Scarabeo Edizioni D'Arte.

Page 119: The Three of Coins, Visconti Tarots, Lo Scarabeo Edizioni D'Arte.

Page 122: The Four of Wands, Visconti Tarots, Lo Scarabeo Edizioni D'Arte.

Page 125: The Five of Cups, Visconti Tarots, Lo Scarabeo Edizioni D'Arte.

page 128: The Six of Swords, Visconti Tarots, Lo Scarabeo Edizioni D'Arte.

Page 131: The Seven of Coins, Visconti Tarots, Lo Scarabeo Edizioni D'Arte.

Page 134: The Eight of Cups, Visconti Tarots, Lo Scarabeo Edizioni D'Arte.

Page 137: The Nine of Wands, Visconti Tarots, Lo Scarabeo Edizioni D'Arte.

Page 140: The Ten of Wands, Visconti Tarots, Lo Scarabeo Edizioni D'Arte.

Page 143: The Page of Wands, Visconti Tarots, Lo Scarabeo Edizioni D'Arte.

Page 146: The Knight of Cups Visconti Tarots, Lo Scarabeo Edizioni D'Arte.

Page 149: The Queen of Swords, Visconti Tarots, Lo Scarabeo Edizioni D'Arte.

Page 152: The King of Coins, Visconti Tarot, Lo Scarabeo Edizioni D'Arte.

Pages 22, 36-59, 61, 62, 63, 65 67, 69, 71, 73, 75, 77, 79, 81, 83, 85, 87, 89, 91, 93, 95, 97, 99, 101, 103, 105, 107, 109, 114-115, 117-118, 120-121, 123-124, 126-127, 129-130, 132-133, 135-136, 138-139, 141-142, 144-145, 147-148, 150-151, 153-154 Cards illustrated by Emma Garner from *The Art of Tarot* (book and tarot deck) by Liz Dean, Cico Books.

Art
Hebrew letter art on pages 24, 25, and 27 by Samantha Wilson.
Aleph card on page 27 by Mandy Pritty.

Particular thanks go to Sasha Fenton and Jonathan Dee, for their help in sourcing Tarot cards.

THE MYSTERY OF THE TAROT

INDEX

Page numbers in italics refer to captions

The Aces 9, *14*, *15*, *20*, *111*, 112, 113–15
Alasia, Silvana *16*, *17*
Aliette, J.-B. 16, *24*, *25*
angels 94, 95, 96, 106
animals
    ass 30, 86
    birds 72, 74, 75
    crayfish 29, 102
    dog *17*, 28, 30, 66
    dragon 29, 86
    horse 29, 80
    lion 29, 88–9
    monkey 30, 86
    snake 28, 84
    wolf *17*, 28, 102
The Art of the Tarot deck 7
astrology 7, 20–3, 140
Attendolo, Muzio 91

Belgium 10
Belline deck *11*
Bembo, Bonifacio 9
Bolognese pack 9
Builders of the Adytum 19
Burns Parke, Jesse 19

Camphausen, Rufus *26*
Case, Paul Foster 19
Celtic Cross spread 45–7
Celtic influences 15
The Chariot 18, 21, 23, 26, 29, 80–1
Charles VI deck *8*, 76
cherub 104
China 14
Colman Smith, Pamela 18, *19*, 33, 110

color, meaning 30–1, 72
Constant, A.L. (Eliphas Levi) *16*, 17, 27
Conver, Nicolas *10*, 33
cosmic cards *23*, 100–5
Court cards 7, *13*, 110–11, 143–54
Covelluzzo, Giovanni di 14
The Crocodile *see* Fool
Crowley, Aleister 18–19
Crystal Tarot *33*, 94

Death 21, 23, 27, 92–3
decks
    choosing 32–3
    number of cards 9, 14, 62, 110
    shuffling and cutting 35
    types 7, 8–9, 110
de Gebelin, A.C. 16
De Leon, Moses 24
De Troyes, Christien de 15
Della Rocca, Carlo *6*
Devil 21, 23, 25, 27, 96–7
Dodal, Jean *10*
Douglas, Alfred 28, 64, 91

Edmond, Magus *11*
Egypt 11, 12, 16–19
The Eights 112, 134–6
elements 20, 21–2, 111, 143, 146, 149, 152
The Emperor 15, 21, 23, 26, 64, 74–5
The Empress 21, 26, 31, 72–3
Etteilla Tarot 16, *24*, *25*, 83, 91

Face cards *see* Court cards
Fame *see* Judgment
Fate *see* Wheel of Fortune
figure-of-eight 63–5, 68, 88, 134
The Fives *110*, 112, 125–7
Florentine deck 9, *20*, 107
Fool (Crocodile/Jester)
    dogs 28, 30, 66
    element 20
    Hebrew *24*, 26, *27*
    Marseilles deck *10*
    meaning *11*, 31, 62–3, 66–7
    planetary association 21
Fortitude *see* Strength
The Fours 112, 122–4
France 10, *11*, *14*, 16, *25*, 33
Furata, Koji 33
future, questions 53–60

geometric design 7, 32, 110
Germany 10, 33
Golden Dawn, Order 18–19, 20, 27, 33, 111
Great Mother 73
Greene, Liz 33
Grigonneur deck 8–9, 76

Hanged Man 20, 21, 27, 90–1
Harris, Lady Frieda 19
Heart and Head spread 38–9
Hebrew *17*, *18*, 24, 26–7, 33, 81
The Hermit 21, 23, 26, 28, 63, 64, 84–5
The Hierophant 21, 23, 26, 33, 76–7
High Priest *see* Hierophant
High Priestess 9, 15, 21, 26, 31, 33, 70–1

158

INDEX

history 6, 7, 8–9, 10–19
Holy Grail legend 15
Horseshoe spread 51–2
House of God *see* The Tower

I Ching 34
India 12, 15
interpreting the cards 6, 7
    Court cards 110–12
    major arcana 18, 26–7
    minor arcana 18, 21–2
    pip cards 112, 114–42
    problems 61
    reversed cards 64
intuitive readings 35, 61
Iris 94, 102
Italian decks
    cardinal virtues 83
    The Emperor 75
    history 9, 10, 11, 12–13, 14
    The Magician 68

Japan 33
Judgment *19*, 20–1, 27, 106–7
Jung, Carl 21
Justice *8*, 21, 23, 26, 82–3

kabbala 11, 16–18, 24–7, 48,
    81, 90
Kaplan, Stuart R. 33
The Kings 112, 152–4
The Knights *12, 13*, 112, 146–8
Knights Templar 13
Korea 14

laying the cards 7, 32–61
Levi, Eliphas *16*, 17, 27
lightning 98, 99
Liguna Piedmont Tarot *14*
love 37, 39, 78–9
The Lovers *19*, 21, 23, 26, 78–9

The Magician (Magus) 13, 15,
    21, 26, 31, 63, 68–9
major arcana
    animals 28–30

cards 66–109
interpreting 7, 18, 62–5
kabbala 17, 25, 26–7
using 34, 38, 40
Malory, Sir Thomas 15
Marseilles deck
    Ace of Cups *111*
    The Fool *10*
    Knight of Swords *13*
    The Magician 68
    production *10*, 30, 33
    Queen of Pentacles *32*
    The World 64, 108
Mathers, Samuel Liddell
    (later MacGregor) 18, 19
meditative readings 35, 48
minchiate decks 9, *20*, 107
minor arcana
    Court cards 143–54
    elements 21–2
    interpreting 7, 18, 110–12
    kabbala link 17, 27
    origins 11, 14–15
    pip cards 113–42
Moakley, Gertrude 107
money 37, 51–2, 58
month ahead spread 56–7
The Moon *16*, 21, 23, *23*, 27,
    28, 29, 102–3
Moon, Beth *19*
Mythic Tarot 33

naipes / naib 14
negative cards 64
Newell, Tricia 33
The Nines 64, 112, 137–9
number of cards 9, 14, 62, 110
numbered (pip) cards 7, 18,
    32, 33, 110, 112

occult societies 16–19
Oswald Wirth Tarot *18*

The Pages 9, 112, 143–5
Papess *see* High Priestess
past, resolving 40–1

past, present and future
    spread 42–4
personality 81, 104
pip cards 7, 18, 32, 33, 110, 112
Pitois, Jean-Baptiste 16
planets 20–1
playing cards *13*, 14, 33, 111
Pope *see* Hierophant
preparation 34–5

The Queens *32*, 112, 149–51

reading the cards 34, 35, 61
relationships 36, 39, 64, 78–9
religion
    Buddhism 86, 99
    Christianity 6, 10, 12, 13,
    15, 76, 134, 137, 140
    Hebrew 11, 17, 107, 140
    Hindu 15, 99, 125
    Taoism 137
relocation 49–50
reversed cards 64
Rider Waite deck
    The Chariot 80
    Death 92
    The Devil 96
    The Empress 72, 73
    Five of Pentacles *110*
    Judgment 106
    The Lovers *19*
    The Magician 68
    The Moon 102
    Nine of Cups 63–4
    publication 18, 19, 33, 110
    Strength 88
    The Sun 31
    The World 108
Romanies 12–13
Romany method 111

Sacred Rose deck 30, 33, 72
The Scales *see* Justice
sephira 17–18, 24–6, 27, 48
The Sevens 112, 131–3
Sharman-Burke, Juliet 33

159

Sherman, Johanna 33
shuffling the cards 35
Silver Star, Order of 19
The Sixes 112, 128–31
Skeleton *see* Death
social life 54, 58
Spain 14, *24, 25*
Sphinx *17, 18*
spreads
   Celtic cross 45–7
   heart and head 38–9
   horseshoe 51–2
   month ahead 56–7
   past, present and future
   42–4
   star 40–1
   three-card 36–7
   tree of life 48–50
   varying 34
   week ahead 58–60
   year ahead 53–5
Star 21, 23, 27, *33*, 100–1
star spread 40–1
Strength 21, 23, 26, 29, 63, 64,
   88–9
suits 110
Sun *6*, 21, *23*, 27, 31, 104–5
Switzerland *12*, 33
swords 31, 82, 86, 106
symbolism 7, 12, 20–31

Temperance 21, 23, 27, 83,
   94–5
The Tens 112, 140–2
Thoth deck 18–19

three-card spreads 36–7
The Threes 112, 119–21
Tilley, Roger 13
Time *see* The Hermit
timing of readings 22–3, 34
The Tower 21, *25*, 27, 98–9
The Traitor *see* Hanged Man
travel 37
Tree of Life 18, 24–5, *26*, 81,
   90, 140
Tree of Life spread 48–50
Trevisan, Elisabetta *33*
Trumpet *see* Judgment
trumps (triumphs) 14
The Twos 63, 112, 116–18

Ukiyoe Tarot 33
Universe *see* The World

Van Leewen, Apolonia *26*
Venetian decks 9, 14
Visconti-Sforza Tarot
   The Chariot 80
   cosmic cards *23*
   Death 92
   The Devil 96
   The Emperor 74, 75
   The Empress 72
   The Fool 66
   The Hanged Man 91
   The Hermit 84
   High Priestess 31, 71
   history 7, 9, 11, 33
   Judgment 106
   Justice 82, 83

   Knight of Cups *13*
   The Lovers 78
   The Magician 68
   The Moon 102
   The Star 100
   Strength 88
   The Sun 104
   The Tower 98
   Wheel of Fortune 86
   The World 108
Visconti Tarot 9

Waite, Arthur Edward 6, 18,
   19, 33, 111
The Waldenses 12–13
water 94, 95, 99, 100, 106
websites 160
week ahead spread 58–60
Wegmuller, Walter 33, *33*
Westcott, William Wynn 18
Wheel of Fortune 15, 21, 26,
   29, 30, 64, 86–7
Woodman, William Robert 18
work 36, 37, 38, 42–3, 46, 54,
   56–7
The World 18, 21, 27, 64,
   108–9

year ahead spread 53–5
Yeats, W.B. 19
Yohai, Shimon ben 24

Zigeuner Tarot 33, *33*
zodiac, signs 22–3, 140
The Zohar 24–5

Acknowledgments

With thanks to all at Cico Books, and to David Fordham for his creative design.
Thank you to my family and special friends, for your interest and support.
And to Jonathan Dee, Kay Curtis, Bernard Holden, Daphne Roubini and Elizabeth
Cunningham, for making me laugh.